Foreword

The period spanning 1060-1088 was a time
and turmoil for the English nation. In the sc
years, a single event may loom large in the public consciousness. the
Battle of Hastings and the subsequent ascension of William. However,
this guide will introduce you to the broader perspective of Anglo-Saxon
and Norman England throughout the years 1060-1088.

From the twilight years of Edward the Confessor's reign, the book
proceeds to the seismic shift that was the Norman Conquest, and further
into the reign of William and his early successors. It weaves together the
political, social, and economic threads of this time, providing a cohesive
and enlightening tapestry of a critical period in English history.

This guide is designed for everyone, whether a student preparing
for an examination or a history enthusiast aiming to deepen their
understanding. The language is clear, the narrative is engaging, and the
content is underpinned by meticulous research and a commitment to
historical accuracy.

Contents

Introduction – Why is this an important topic?

At first glance a study of 'Anglo-Saxon and Norman England, c1060-1088' can seem quite dull. Whilst most people are already familiar with the battles of 1066 and the various claimants to the English throne, the inner workings of Saxon and Norman society are less known. The year 1066 was a pivotal moment in English, British, European and, potentially, world history. For as this book demonstrates, prior to William of Normandy's conquest life in England was very distinct from its neighbours on the continent.

By successfully conquering England William changed the course of English history, bringing with him French language, French traditions and a new French upper class that would dominate the Anglo-Saxon 'English' population for many years to come. This topic serves to demonstrate just how significant 1066 was, not just because it was a year of battles and claimants but because it set English history on a new course. Arguably, had William been unsuccessful and Harold Godwinson held the English throne, history would have travelled a completely different path absent of the famous kings who followed William I.

So, if you are either a teacher picking up this book as a handy go to for key information to teach your students, or if you are in fact a student using this book to support your revision remember to view this as a narrative of how England transformed as consequence of the Norman Conquest.

Key Topic 1 – Anglo-Saxon society and the Norman Conquest, 1060-1066

This key topic sets the scene by outlining what life was like in Anglo-Saxon England before focusing upon the events of 1066.

1.1 - Anglo-Saxon society

The King, The Earls and The Witan

In order to understand the impact of changes which were imposed by William we must first look at what life was like prior to the Norman Conquest.

In Anglo-Saxon society the king was regarded as the most senior individual in the land. In the 1060s Edward the Confessor was the king of England. As an Anglo-Saxon king Edward possessed a number of important powers such as:

- Creating new laws
- Granting land to followers
- Removing land from people as punishment
- Making decisions on taxation
- Raising a peasant army known as the 'Fyrd'

The king was regarded as being chosen by God to lead Anglo-Saxon England, which gave him a certain amount of religious authority which justified the numerous powers he held.

However Anglo-Saxon kings also faced several issues and challenges, one of which was 'Danelaw'. This term was used to describe the northern half of England which had much more Viking-like traditions. Whilst still the ruler of this area, it was important for the Anglo-Saxon king to allow the population here a little more independence. For example, taxation was often lower, and law and order was often more flexible.

The Witan was a council which provided Anglo-Saxon kings with advice. The king chose when to call the Witan to advise him, what they would be advising him on and who was appointed to the Witan; he could choose to ignore the advice of the Witan. Whilst often a source of support the Witan could also pose a king with problems. For instance, if an Anglo-Saxon king was weak or lacking in authority the Witan could impose its will upon him, potentially controlling him in the process.

Anglo-Saxon kings also faced this problem with individual Earls. From time to time the authority of kings was challenged by powerful Earls who commanded more influence, wealth and land than the king. Earls were the most important individuals in Anglo-Saxon society after the king and controlled large areas of England on behalf of the monarch. These were known as Earldoms. Within their Earldoms, Earls possessed some powers similar to those of the king:

- Collecting taxes from the earldom
- Dispensing law and order in their earldom
- Raising their own warriors for battle known as Thegns

If an earl possessed a particularly large earldom then they became extremely powerful. In some cases, they were even able to directly challenge the authority of the king.

Key Points:

- The king was the most important individual in Anglo-Saxon England
- The king possessed a number of powers such as law making and tax collection
- The king was 'appointed by god'
- Danelaw posed unique challenges for kings due to its Viking traditions and cultural differences
- The Witan advised the king on a variety of important matters
- Earls were also very powerful, controlling Earldoms and ruling land on behalf of the king
- Earls collected taxes and distributed land to Thegns
- Some Earls had enough power to rival the authority of the king

The Saxon Social System

During this time period society could be separated into two parts: 'secular' and 'non-secular'.

'Non-Secular' refers to The Church, which was a very powerful institution at this time. Bishops were at the top of The Church and controlled large areas of Church land and formed part of The Witan. Members of The Church could write, most people in England could not, so they provided the king with this service. Lower down in church society were priests, who were not well educated and were very much like peasants as they often farmed the land. Monks and Nuns also lived as part of the general community. The Anglo-Saxon Church was very resistant to the religious changes taking place in areas such as France, and therefore Anglo-Saxon Christianity was very different to religion on the continent.

'Secular' on the other hand refers to everything non-religious. Secular society can be broadly described as a social hierarchy. At the top was The King, and beneath him sat The Earls. Beneath Earls were Thegns. Thegns were also nobles but less powerful than Earls, they controlled land on behalf of their Earl and performed certain duties on a local level such as tax collecting. There was also a sub-group of Thegns known as King's Thegns. These individuals were similar to regular Thegns except they operated in areas directly controlled by The King. Nobles made up approximately 10 percent of Saxon society. Around 80 percent of the population were farmers, 10 percent of whom were known as Ceorls. Ceorls were freemen who owned small areas of land which they farmed. The remaining 70 percent were Peasants, their main duty was to farm their local lord's land and complete any other jobs as requested. The final 10 percent of Saxon society was made up of Slaves. Slaves were not free and possessed no land. Every aspect of a slave's life was controlled by their master. Estimates suggest that the population of Anglo-Saxon England amounted to around 2 million people in 1060.

In times of war, Kings could call upon Earls and Thegns to fight for them as a professional and well-equipped fighting force. Kings would also call up Ceorls and Peasants to fight as part of the Fyrd in times of great need.

Key Points:

- Bishops were the most influential members of The Church and made up part of the Witan
- Many churchmen were highly educated and could write, so they often worked for kings and Earls by writing laws and keeping records
- Priests were lower down in the church and played a similar role in day-to-day life as peasants
- Secular refers to anything not linked to religion
- The King was at the top of secular society
- Next in secular society were Earls who controlled earldoms on behalf of kings
- Thegns were given land by Earls and were beneath them in the social hierarchy
- Beneath Thegns were Ceorls
- Peasants made up around 70 percent of society and were the next step down in the hierarchy
- Slaves were at the bottom of society and had no freedom

Government, Law and Economy

Earldoms were divided into shires. Each shire was divided into hundreds, a hundred being an area of land covering 120 acres. Each hundred was divided into tithings. A tithing was 10 households.

Anglo-Saxon England had a complex and effective system of governance. Although the king was at the top of society, he relied heavily on his Earl to maintain control in their earldoms. Local governments ensured that the king's wishes were followed, and that law and order was maintained in each shire. Shire Reeves (Sheriffs) were the king's representative on a local level. The Shire Reeve judged issues of law and order at the shire court, was responsible for maintaining the defences of the shire and for collecting taxes. The geld tax was a tax based on land, but Edward the Confessor rarely used this. The king issued commands to his shire reeves through writs.

Law and order in Anglo-Saxon England relied heavily upon people regulating one another's behaviour in a local area. Collective responsibility meant that if a one person in a tithing committed a crime then the rest were responsible for bringing him to court or else, they too, would suffer punishment. This encouraged people to monitor law and order in their community. If anyone in the community requested help to track down a criminal this was known as the Hue and Cry. Shire Reeves could also issue a Hue and Cry. In Anglo-Saxon England everything had a price, including someone's life. If someone was murdered then the killer would have to pay the victim's family money, the amount depended on their station in society. This was known as the Wergild (Blood Price). If this was not paid then a Blood Feud would commence.

The Anglo-Saxon economy was very strong in the 1060s, which no doubt made the English throne so attractive to the various claimants in 1066. Crop farming and the rearing of livestock was particularly efficient due to the English climate. Anglo-Saxon England also had efficient trade links with its European neighbours, especially Scandinavia, modern-day France and Belgium. All this, coupled with the fact that there was a highly effective tax system and that the coinage held its value, meant that the English crown was in a strong position financially.

Burhs were Anglo-Saxon fortified towns. Originally introduced by Alfred the Great of Wessex as a means to protect the rural population from Viking attacks, burhs acted as the main town in each shire. If a shire was attacked people could flee to the local burh for protection behind its fortified walls. All trade had to take place in burhs, which was of course taxed.

Key Points:

- Earldoms were split into shires, shires were split into hundreds and hundreds were split into tithings
- Anglo-Saxon England was well governed
- Kings relied on their Earls to help them govern the land
- Shire Reeves were the King's representatives, operating at a local level
- Shire Reeves collected tax
- The Geld Tax was a tax based on land but Edward the Confessor rarely used this
- Collective Responsibility meant that members of a tithing were responsible for ensuring that one another obeyed the law
- A Hue and Cry was when members of a tithing hunted for a criminal who was part of their tithing
- A Blood Feud started when a member of one family murdered a member of another
- To stop a Blood Feud, the offending family had to pay the Wergild (Blood Price)
- Anglo-Saxon England had a strong farming economy and an effective tax system
- Burhs were fortified towns and protected large amounts of people from Viking attack

1.2 - The last years of Edward the Confessor

Edward the Confessor

Edward the confessor ruled England from 1042-1066 and was the son of King Ethelred the Unready and Emma of Normandy. He succeeded his half-brother Halfacnut to the throne, who was the son of King Cnut the Great a Norwegian Viking) and Emma of Normandy. His reign signalled the end of Danish-Viking rule of England, which had started in 1016. Historians disagree on Edward as a ruler, with some regarding him as weak and ineffective whilst others argue he was energetic, resourceful and, at times, ruthless. Edward spent most of his life living in exile in Normandy, birthplace of his mother, whilst Cnut and then Halfacnut ruled England.

Edward returned to England in 1041 whilst his half-brother was still king and, when Halfacnut died, he took the throne in 1042. Edward relied heavily on Earl Godwin, and in 1045 he married Edith of Wessex, daughter of Earl Godwin.

Key Points:

- Edward the Confessor ruled from 1042-1066
- Edward spent a number of years living in Normandy whilst Danish kings ruled over England
- Edward's reputation as a ruler is mixed
- Edward was reliant on a powerful Earl called Godwin and he even married Godwin's daughter Edith

The House of Godwin

Earl Godwin was an extremely important individual and although he died before the 1060s it is crucial that his life and legacy are understood.

Although Earl Godwin's origins are somewhat mysterious, it is believed he was the son of an Anglo-Saxon Thegn called Wulfnoth Cild. During the reign of King Cnut Godwin's rank increased significantly and by 1018 he was an earl. It was possible in Anglo-Saxon society for individuals to move through the societal structure and increase their rank. By 1020 Godwin was the Earl of Wessex and in 1023 he married a Danish noble called Gytha. In 1040 he supported Edward's claim to the English throne and did so again in 1042. Godwin's daughter, Edith, was married to King Edward in 1045.

In 1051, Earl Godwin was ordered by King Edward to punish the people of Dover after they had assaulted a nobleman from Normandy, the area of France where Edward had spent his exile. Earl Godwin, like many nobles, was growing tired of the influence of Norman nobles at Edward's court and he therefore refused to punish the people of Dover for their actions.

Following this incident, Godwin and his sons were banished from England. He, along with his wife Gytha and sons Sweyn, Tostig and Gyrth sought refuge in Flanders. His sons Leofwine and Harold fled to Dublin. In the following year however Godwin and his family returned to England with a large armed force, forcing King Edward to restore the earldom of Wessex to Godwin.

The term House of Godwin refers to Earl Godwin's family, which was arguably the most powerful family in Anglo-Saxon England during this period. They had much support and potentially held more respect and power than Edward himself. Upon Earl Godwin's death in 1053 his son Harold became the Earl of Wessex – his eldest son Sweyn had died the previous year.

Key Points:

- Earl Godwin was an extremely powerful individual in Anglo-Saxon England
- Godwin's daughter was married to the King Edward the Confessor
- The House of Godwin is used to refer to Earl Godwin and his family
- In 1051 the House of Godwin was exiled from England
- They were able to return in 1052 and force King Edward to restore all of their land
- Earl Godwin's ability to force Edward to return his land proves that he was as, if not more, powerful than his king
- Harold Godwinson inherited Godwin's main earldom, Wessex, in 1053

Harold and Tostig

Harold Godwinson (named Godwin-son as he was the son of Godwin) became the Earl of Hereford in 1058. Earl Godwin's other sons also achieved the rank of Earl. Tostig Godwinson was made Earl of Northumbria, Gyrth Godwinson was made Earl of East Anglia, and Leofwine Godwinson became the Earl of Kent. The House of Godwin controlled all the earldoms of Anglo-Saxon England except for one, Mercia, which was controlled by Earl Edwin.

Harold Godwinson positioned himself as Edward's most trusted advisor, however Edward likely felt pressured to allow this due to the immense power Harold and his brothers held. Two important events concerning the sons of Godwin occurred in the 1060s. In 1064 Harold was shipwrecked in Ponthieu, modern day Belgium. Events following Harold's shipwreck are unclear, largely due to the fact that Norman and Saxon chroniclers (writers) offer conflicting accounts of what happened, but they nevertheless proved to be extremely important; this will be explored in a later section.

In 1065 a less debated event occurred involving both Harold and Tostig. As Earl of Northumbria, Tostig failed to recognise the traditions of Danelaw (the northern parts of England that followed Viking customs) and alienated much of the local population. He taxed the people of Northumbria heavily, something that they were not used to in Danelaw. It was also rumoured that Tostig had a hand in the murder of several members of leading Northumbrian families, and, in late 1064, Tostig had Gamal, son of Orm, and Ulf, son of Dolfin, assassinated when they visited him. Not only was Tostig disliked for his heavy-handed approach, but he was also from the south and this no doubt further frustrated the Northumbrian people. In 1065 a rebel force attacked York, killing many of Tostig's advisors and supporters. Tostig was outlawed and Morcar, younger brother of Edwin (Earl of Mercia), was declared as the new Earl of Northumbria.

King Edward sent Harold to negotiate with the rebels, which resulted in an agreement that Morcar remained Earl of Northumbria and that Tostig should return south. Tostig was unable to come to terms with this and was eventually exiled from England. It is also likely that Harold accepted these terms as at this time he was probably getting ready to claim the throne once Edward died, who was by now an elderly man. Having the support of both Northumbria and Mercia would strengthen Harold's claim significantly.

Key Points:

- Harold Godwinson was a powerful individual like his father Earl Godwin
- In 1064 Harold was shipwrecked in Northern Europe
- In 1065 Earl Tostig was replaced as Earl of Northumbria by Morcar
- Earl Tostig was accused by the people of Northumbria of numerous crimes including murder
- Tostig did not understand the North due to its tradition of Danelaw
- Danelaw refers to the Northern parts of England that had many Viking customs
- Tostig was overthrown by the people of Northumbria
- Harold was Tostig's brother but supported Morcar as the new Earl of Northumbria
- Tostig could not agree to this arrangement and was eventually exiled from England

1.3 - The rival claimants for the throne

Edgar Aethling

Edward the Confessor died on January 5th, 1066. With no son to succeed him, and no daughter to marry to a potential suitor, many individuals argued their claim to the English throne; as to who should be the next king, that was the decision of the Witan.

The closest living relative to Edward was Edgar, often referred to as Edgar Aethling (Aethling meaning 'throne-worthy') demonstrating that he was potentially regarded as a genuine candidate to succeed Edward as king. Edgar's father was Edward the Exile, son of King Edmund Ironside who lost the English throne to Cnut in 1016. Edward the Exile spent much of his life in exile in the Kingdom of Hungary and it is here that he married Agatha, with whom he had two daughters and a son named Edgar. In 1056 King Edward the Confessor discovered Edward the Exile was alive and called him back to England. Upon Edward the Exile's return he was named by King Edward as his heir, due to the fact that he was directly descended from an Anglo-Saxon king. However, Edward the Exile died in 1057 shortly after arriving in England, before he was even able to meet King Edward.

Edgar now remained as the only living male member of the royal dynasty aside from the king himself, however it does not appear as though King Edward made much effort to secure his great-nephew's position as his heir. Edgar most likely inherited the Aethling title from his father, rather than being assigned it by King Edward. At the time of Edward's death Edgar was only 15, had no leadership experience, no soldiers and very little money. It is no surprise that the Witan did not vote for him to be the next Anglo-Saxon King.

Key Points:

- King Edward died on 5th January 1066
- In Anglo-Saxon England the Witan, the King's Council, chose the next King
- Edgar was the closest living male relative of Edward the Confessor
- Edgar's father had been named heir but died under suspicious circumstances
- Edgar had a strong blood claim but was only 15 years old
- The lack of experience, lack of an army and lack of finances meant that Edgar was not chosen by members of The Witan

William of Normandy

Another, more distant, relative to King Edward was William of Normandy. William was King Edward's first cousin once removed. It was with William whom King Edward had spent time in exile during the reigns of Cnut the Great, Harold Harefoot and Harthacnut.

William was the illegitimate son of Robert Duke of Normandy. William's illegitimacy, coupled with his youth, meant that succeeding his father as Duke of Normandy was fraught with difficulty. Norman nobles battled for control of William during his youth, but in 1047 William defeated a rebellion and began to establish himself in his own right. Throughout the 1050s and into the 1060s William continued to fight for complete dominance over Normandy. William argued that King Edward had promised to give him the throne after his death. This promise would have been made either during the time Edward spent in Normandy as an exile, or years later whilst he was King of England.

William also claimed that Harold Godwinson swore an oath to support his claim to the throne. This apparently occurred during the time that Harold was shipwrecked in Ponthieu, as he was then taken to Normandy as a prisoner. Norman chroniclers state that Harold swore on religious relics that he would support William's claim. Anglo-Saxon chroniclers on the other hand claim this did not happen and instead suggest that this was a lie used by William to further justify his claim to the throne.

Key Points:

- William of Normandy was a distant cousin of King Edward
- Throughout his life William had fought to maintain control of his lands in Normandy
- William claimed that he had been promised the throne by Edward
- William also claimed Harold Godwinson had sworn an oath to support his claim to the English throne

Harald Hardrada

As previously mentioned, between the years 1016 and 1042 England was ruled by Danish Vikings. Another contender, Harald Hardrada, claimed the English throne as he was a descendant of King Cnut. Hara d was a warrior of great renowned as he had spent many years fighting in the East as a mercenary, during which time he amassed great wealth. Upon his return to Scandinavia, he established himself as King of Norway, and engaged in numerous attempts to seize the throne of Denmark.

Harald's relationship to the throne of England is the most complicated of the four. For one, he had no direct link to King Edward. Instead, Harald's connection was that his great grandfather was Cnut the Great – King of England. His father Magnus was supposed to inherit the throne from Halfacnut, but Edward claimed it before Magnus was able to do so.

The strong tradition of Danelaw in the North of England also encouraged Harald in his claim as he felt confident that Viking descendants would join him once he started to capture land in Northumbria.

Key Points:

- Harald Hardrada claimed the throne as his Great Grandfather had once been the King of England
- Harald's father had been promised the throne, but Edward the Confessor claimed it first
- Harald was a famous and wealthy warrior and was the King of Norway
- Harald was encouraged in his claim by Tostig Godwinson

Harold Godwinson

When King Edward the Confessor died Harold was at his bedside; afterwards Harold claimed that he had been named as heir to the throne. As the most powerful Earl in England Harold held much respect amongst the members of The Witan. He controlled Wessex, the most powerful English Earldom, had siblings who controlled Kent and East Anglia and had even forged an alliance with Edwin (Earl of Mercia) and his brother Morcar (Earl of Northumbria) when he exiled Tostig in 1065. In 1063 Harold had shown his military might when he defeated the Welsh and had amassed such wealth and prestige that he was regarded as King Edward's right hand man. It is therefore unsurprising that he was elected to be the next king on January 6th, 1066, and crowned the very same day.

Harold immediately faced threats towards his rule. No doubt aware of William of Normandy's desire to claim the throne for himself, Harold raised the southern Fyrd and stationed it towards the south coast. His brother Tostig began raiding along the south eastern coast before sailing north towards Northumbria, and all the while Harold waited for a Norman invasion that did not come. Forced to disband the Fyrd so that the men could harvest their crops, Harold returned to London where he received news of an invasion in the North.

Key Points:

- Harold Godwinson was promised the throne by King Edward
- Harold was the most powerful person in England and was elected by The Witan on January 6th, 1066
- The Fyrd was raised to protect England from an invasion by William of Normandy
- Tostig Godwinson raided the south eastern coast of England before heading north
- Harold had to disband the Fyrd when William's invasion did not come

The Battle of Gate Fulford

Tostig Godwinson's small fleet of ships made its way up the coast of England until it reached Northumbria, where it suffered defeat to Earl Morcar. Following a brief stay in Scotland, Tostig joined forces with the invading army of Harald Hardrada. The combined forces sailed up the Humber Estuary and along the River Ouse towards York in September 1066, leaving their ships at Ricall before being confronted by Edwin and Morcar near the village of Fulford on September 20th.

Edwin, the Earl of Mercia, arrived at York with an army to support Morcar, his brother and Earl of Northumbria. For this to have occurred it is more than likely that word of Harald Hardrada's intention to invade had reached England and that the Norwegian invasion was not necessarily a surprise. The two armies met near the village of Fulford, to the south of York, at a place called Germany Beck. Germany Beck was a tributary (a smaller river joining a larger river) to the River Ouse. Edwin and Morcar lined their forces up on the northern side of the bank, forming a shield wall. A shield wall was a common tactic in Anglo-Saxon England. Soldiers would stand side by side in a tight formation, overlaying their shields with the people either side. This created a wooden wall which was hard to breakthrough, and behind it soldiers carried swords and spears which they would then thrust at the enemy. To the right of the Anglo-Saxon force was the River Ouse and to the left a large swampy area. Edwin and Morcar's army totalled around 4,000 to 5,000 men.

Harald Hardrada's invasion force numbered around 10,000 men, but at the battle it is believed only 6,000 were deployed as the rest were guarding the ships. Hardrada's army was marching towards York along three routes and was therefore stretched out over a number of miles. When he arrived on the south bank of Germany Beck his army had the higher ground, but the Anglo-Saxons had a clear advantage as Hardrada's full force had not yet arrived. His force formed a shield wall opposite that of Edwin and Morcar, keeping his most experienced fighters to the rear in reserve, and the Anglo-Saxons attacked.

Unfortunately for Edwin and Morcar their army was unable to make the most of their initial advantage, which gave Hardrada opportunity to coordinate a counterattack. Using his most experienced troops, which he had kept in reserve, Hardrada flanked (moved around to attack the sides and rear) the Anglo-Saxon army. Despite still being outnumbered the Norwegian invaders were able to force the Anglo-Saxons back, splitting Edwin and Morcar's army in two. As more and more of Hardrada's men arrived on the battlefield the Anglo-Saxons began to retreat.

Edwin and Morcar survived the battle, and Harald Hardrada celebrated the victory by marching to York and forcing the city to surrender. Likely at the request of Tostig, who intended to reclaim his title as Earl of Northumbria once Hardrada was king, York was not looted and instead the Norwegian army went to a place called Stamford Bridge. It was here that they intended to wait for hostages before heading southwards to capture more territory.

Key Points:

- Tostig Godwinson joined forces with Harald Hardrada's army of Norwegian invaders
- The two men led their army in battle against Edwin, Earl of Mercia, and Morcar, Earl of Northumbria
- The Anglo-Saxon and Norwegian armies met on September 20th at what became known as the Battle of Fulford
- At first the Anglo-Saxons had an advantage as not all of the Norwegian soldiers had arrived, but they could not make any gains
- Harald Hardrada used a flanking manoeuvre to separate Edwin and Morcar's army in two
- As more Norwegian soldiers arrived The Anglo-Saxon army was forced to retreat

The Battle of Stamford Bridge

King Harold Godwinson was in the south of England when he discovered what had happened at The Battle of Fulford. He now had to act swiftly before the Norwegian invaders were able to conquer more land, so he gathered an army and marched north to meet them in battle. Over the course of just 5 days Harold Godwinson's army marched 185 miles, catching Harald Hardrada and Tostig Godwinson completely by surprise.

Following their victory at Fulford, Harald Hardrada and his Norwegian army were celebrating at Stamford Bridge. They did not expect to be attacked as they had just defeated Anglo-Saxon forces in the North and were so far from Harold Godwinson in the south that they were confident they would not be disturbed. Harald was in fact so confident of his safety that he had ordered his army to leave all their armour with the ships, where he also stationed a large bulk of his forces. Nevertheless, on September 25th an Anglo-Saxon force led by King Harold completely surprised the unprepared Norwegian invaders at Stamford Bridge.

No doubt surprised by the sudden arrival of the Anglo-Saxon army, Hardrada sent riders to request reinforcements from the soldiers whom he had left to protect the ships. Vastly outnumbered, the only thing separating Harald Hardrada's army from Harold Godwinson's was the River Derwent and a narrow wooden bridge. It is said that the Anglo-Saxon army wars held up on this bridge for some time by a giant Norwegian warrior wielding a giant axe, who killed approximately 40 soldiers before being stabbed from below by an Anglo-Saxon soldier who had floated under the bridge in a barrel. During this time Hardrada had managed to gather his force into a shield wall.

Godwinson led his army across the bridge and formed a shield wall opposite Hardrada's much thinner line. Despite being outnumbered and under armoured the Norwegian army was able to hold its line for a number of hours, no doubt hoping for reinforcements to soon appear. Unfortunately for Hardrada his shield wall began to break; Anglo-Saxon forces forced their way through the Norwegian line, surrounding small pockets of enemy soldiers. Completely outflanked, the Norwegian forces began to crumble and when Harald Hardrada was struck in the eye with an arrow the battle was all but lost. Tostig Godwinson was also killed, but the details of his death are not well documented. Reinforcements did eventually arrive under the leadership of Hardrada's prospective son-in-law Eystein Orre, and they did briefly slow the Anglo-Saxon forces in a counterattack which became known as 'Orre's Storm'. Nevertheless, The Anglo-Saxon army was able to press its advantage, annihilating their enemy in the process.

After the battle King Harold Godwinson spared Harald Hardrada's son, Olaf, under the agreement that no Norwegian army ever invade England again. Of the 300 ships that had brought Harald Hardrada's army to England only 24 were needed to take the survivors home. King Harold Godwinson had defeated the Norwegian claimant to his throne, but he now faced a new threat as on September 28th William of Normandy landed on English soil in an attempt to claim the English throne for himself.

Key Points:

- Harold Godwinson force marched his army 185 miles in 5 days to catch the invading army of Harald Hardrada off guard
- The Norwegian army was camped at Stamford Bridge, but Hardrada had left a number of men and all of his soldiers' armour with his fleet of ships
- On a wooden bridge across the River Derwent a giant Norwegian soldier was able to hold off the Anglo-Saxon army whilst the Norwegians formed a shield wall
- The soldier killed 40 men but was stabbed from under the bridge and died
- The two armies fought for hours before the Anglo-Saxons gained an advantage

- Tostig Godwinson and Harald Hardrada were eventual y killed
- So many Norwegians died that only 24 of the fleet 300 ships were needed to take the survivors home to Norway

1.4 - The Norman invasion

The Battle of Hastings

Whilst King Harold Godwinson was in the North of England combating the invasion of Harald Hardrada and Tostig Godwinson, William of Normandy was planning his own invasion of England. On September 28th William landed at Pevensey Bay on the south coast of England and set about the construction of a Motte and Bailey castle (a small, wooden, defensive structure) in the ruins of an old Roman fort.

Prior to landing at Pevensey William had spent approximately 9 months preparing his invasion fleet. The ships had to be built from nothing, whilst William also needed begin the long process of gathering supplies and soldiers for his invasion. He allegedly gained the support of Pope Alexander II, only one chronicler actually claims this, and was supposedly given a Papal banner to display during his campaign. William also gathered numerous Lords and Barons to his cause, whom he had promised to reward with land and wealth once he claimed the English crown. Once his fleet of ships was constructed, William was ready to set sail for England; the invasion was, however, delayed by unfavourable weather. William eventually landed in England just three days after King Harold Godwinson had defeated the forces of Harald Hardrada and Tostig Godwinson.

Following the Battle of Stamford Bridge, King Harold Godwinson marched his tired and battle-weary army southwards. Most likely, word of William's invasion reached Harold whilst he was journeying south. When he reached London Harold spent approximately a week resting his soldiers and gathering men of the Fyrd, before setting out to face William in battle. On October 13th the Anglo-Saxon army set up camp on Caldbec Hill, around 8 miles from William's motte and bailey castle at Hastings. William marched his force to meet the Anglo-Saxon army the next day and King Harold established a defensive shield wall on the top of Senlac Hill.

Specifics of the battle are hard to come by due to the fact that Norman and Anglo-Saxon chroniclers give somewhat conflicting accounts of events. It is agreed amongst modern historians that King Harold's army numbered 6,000 to 8,000 and that it was comprised of housecarls and members of the Fyrd. Housecarls were full-time professional soldiers. Their armour consisted of a conical helmet, a mail hauberk (body armour) and a shield. They often carried a two-handed Dane Axe but were also equipped with a short sword, which was very useful in close combat. Harold's army fought entirely on foot and was deployed as a shield wall.

William's army was entirely different in its composition. Numbering around 7,000 to 8,000 men in total, the vast majority of which were professional soldiers, the Norman force was comprised of mounted knights, archers, crossbowmen and foot soldiers. Such a force was unusual in Anglo-Saxon England; battles between Saxons and Vikings had almost always been fought on foot using shield walls, mounted men usually dismounted before battle whilst archers were present but never really used for tactical advantage.

Battle commenced on Saturday 14th October, lasting the entire day and ending in a victory for William. King Harold formed his army in a shield wall at the top of a steep hill, with protection from marshland and woodland on either side. William formed his army in three lines; at the front he deployed his archers and crossbows, in the second line he placed his foot soldiers and in the final line he placed his mounted knights.

William first deployed his archers, who did little damage to the Anglo-Saxons behind their shield wall. Following this William sent in his foot soldiers and then after that his cavalry, but neither advance was able to break Harold's shield wall. There was likely a pause in battle, it was not unusual for forces to tire and the pace of fighting to slow during a battle. During this time William may have devised his plan to break the shield wall. Towards the end of the battle William was able to break the Anglo-Saxon shield wall by using a feigned retreat. This tactic saw the Norman forces pretend to flee, encouraging the Anglo-Saxons to pursue them. Once this occurred William used his cavalry to turn and charge through the gaps in the shield wall created by the Anglo-Saxon's premature victory charge, enabling William's army to defeat many of King Harold's housecarls. Gaps in the shield wall were then filled by less experienced Fyrd soldiers who were easily overpowered by William's soldiers. King Harold, his brothers Gyrth and Leofwine and many other Anglo-Saxon Earls were killed.

Accounts of the battle suggest King Harold was struck in the eye by an arrow, killing him instantly. Specifics of his death aside, the killing of King Harold left the Anglo-Saxons leaderless and their forces began to retreat. William of Normandy was victorious.

Key Points:

- William of Normandy invaded in September 28th whilst King Harold was still in the North of England
- William landed at Pevensey and built a Motte and Bailey castle at Hastings
- William secured support from the Pope and promised land to those individuals supporting his invasion
- King Harold gathered a force of approximately 6,000 to 8,000 men
- William deployed a force of approximately 7,000-8,000
- William's army was made up of archers, crossbowmen, mounted knights and foot soldiers
- The Saxons formed a shield wall at the top of Senlac Hill
- The Normans fought in three lines, attacking in this order, of archers, foot soldiers and then mounted knights
- William struggled to defeat King Harold's army due to the strength of its shield wall
- The Norman's used a false or feigned retreat to trick the Anglo-Saxons into leaving their shield wall
- Many Earls were killed and King Harold was allegedly killed by an arrow in the eye

William's Victory

William of Normandy's victory can be attributed to a number of factors, occurring both during the battle and prior to it. The result was also a consequence of William's excellent leadership, yet it is also possible to argue that errors in King Harold's judgement also played a significant role in the outcome.

Prior to the battle William showed great skill in recognising the importance of establishing a foothold in the south of England. By constructing a castle and raiding the surrounding countryside William successfully provoked King Harold into joining a battle on his terms. It is likely that King Harold did not gather all the forces he had at his disposal due to this provocation. He also neglected to remain in London, or at the very least station himself in a southern burh, again the likelihood here is that he was goaded by William's decision to raid Wessex. Historians tend to agree that King Harold rushed to meet William in battle and that a potentially wiser option may have been to remain in London and gather the full military might of England. Theoretically King Harold could have raised a Fyrd of approximately 14,000 men, as this is roughly how many peasant soldiers he had at his disposal across England. In addition to his royal household troops King Harold also had access the personal fighting forces of his Earls. His decision not to wait in London, or another settlement offering significant protection, in order to gather such a significant force has to be recognised as a failure on his part, and one which undoubtedly contributed greatly towards the outcome at Hastings.

William's ability to provoke King Harold into engaging in battle so soon after Stamford Bridge has to be considered as a contributing factor towards the outcome at the Battle of Hastings. King Harold's army was tired, not a full strength and therefore less likely to defeat William's professional fighting force. Perhaps overconfident from his victory against the formidable Harald Hardrada, King Harold may have felt that a swift response might also catch William by surprise and produce another similar victory. Unfortunately for King Harold William was aware in advance of the approaching Anglo-Saxon army. The Norman force spent the entire night before the battle fully armed and on high alert and on the morning of October 13th William's army was ready to meet King Harold's on the battlefield.

During the battle itself there were pivotal moments which affected the outcome. First and foremost William was a much more experienced military leader. Second, William possessed a very experienced and professional fighting force. Thirdly, the composition of William's army afforded him numerous tactical options. King Harold's army on the other hand was less diverse as it was restricted to fighting in a defensive shield wall formation. The feigned retreat was an extremely significant event in the battle as it enabled William to make the most of of his army's diverse composition whilst simultaneously exposing the vulnerabilities of the Anglo-Saxon shield wall. Nevertheless had the shield wall stood firm and not pursued the falsely retreating Normans then this tactic would have been ineffective. Whether or not the shield wall broke formation due to poor leadership or due to a lack of discipline is unclear, yet the fact remains that in doing so the Anglo-Saxon army lost its defensive advantage and enabled the Normans cavalry to flank them.

The Battle of Hastings showed the superiority of Norman mixed cavalry and infantry tactics over the traditional shield wall approach adopted by Anglo-Saxon and Viking forces. Following the victory William remained near Hastings waiting for the Witan to invite him to be the next king, but this did not happen. Consequently, William of Normandy began the process of securing the kingdom of England through a variety of means.

Key Points:

- King Harold rushed south, tiring his army
- He also neglected to stay in London and gather as large a force as possible
- King Harold's army was restricted to fighting in a defensive shield wall formation

- William raided Wessex, likely provoking King Harold into fighting sooner than he should
- William's army was much more diverse, giving him many tactical options.
- The feigned retreat gave William an advantage in battle
- Either poor Anglo-Saxon leadership or poor discipline amongst the Saxon forces contributed to the success of the feigned retreat

Key Topic 2 – William I: Securing the kingdom, 1066-1087

This key topic focuses upon the methods used by William to establish and then maintain control of England after the Battle of Hastings.

2.1 – Establishing Control

The Submission of the Earls, 1066

In the immediate aftermath of the Battle of Hastings William of Normandy remained close by the battlefield, waiting for the remaining members of the Anglo-Saxon Witan to ask him to become king. Earls Edwin and Morcar and Archbishops Stigand and Ealdred, however, did not do this and instead decided to elect Edgar Aethling to be their next king. William was unsurprisingly furious and set about forcing the Witan to submit to him.

William marched his army northwards along the Kent coastline, securing the port of Dover before heading inland towards Canterbury. Along this route the Norman army forced many towns and villages to submit to William through acts of violence and intimidation.

Edgar, members of the Witan and their combined forces remained behind London's fortifications; here they held quite a strong position. London was well fortified, Edgar had a much stronger claim to the throne and the presence of Earl Edwin and Earl Morcar meant that more than half of England was still directly opposed to William. Furthermore, William's army was now a relatively small force, it was deep in enemy territory and William's claim had essentially been judged by the Witan as being insignificant when they chose to elect Edgar instead. Nevertheless the Norman force continued its route toward London. It was attacked by an Anglo-Saxon force at Southwark, just to the south of London's southern entrance. William easily defeated this enemy, but finding it too difficult to overcome London's defences, William continued his route of destruction and intimidation.

It is at this point that the vulnerabilities of Edgar and the Witan were exposed. Firstly Edgar did not have a strong support base in England, whilst secondly a high number of Anglo-Saxon warriors and nobles had died at the Battle of Hastings; Edgar and the Witan would find it difficult to gather a sizeable force. Furthermore, by staying in London they risked being cut off from reinforcements were William to block routes into the city.

William on the other hand was an effective leader. He had already seized the Royal Treasury at Winchester, crippling Edgar's finances in the process. Additionally, William's ruthless march through southern England meant that many Anglo-Saxons were submitting to him just to avoid death.

Once the Witan and Edgar realised they risked being trapped in London, and seeing no other alternative, they submitted to William at Berkhamstead. On December 25th William was crowned as King of England. Yet despite the Earls submitting to William at Berkhamstead this was not the end of Anglo-Saxon resistance to King William I.

Key Points:

- William thought the Witan would elect him as king after the Battle of Hastings
- Edgar Aethling was elected by the Witan instead
- William decided to force the Witan to name him as king by raiding the English countryside
- Edgar and the Witan were in a strong defensive position in London
- William took a route around London which threatened to cut the Anglo-Saxons off from the rest of England
- Realising that they could not resist William, the members of the Witan submitted to him at Berkhamstead
- William was crowned as King on Christmas Day, 1066

Rewarding Followers

William had now achieved his goal of becoming King of England. But although he was crowned as King William I of England he had by no means secured his new kingdom. If anything, the hard work for William was just beginning.

Prior to his invasion of England William had promised to reward his followers with land and titles in England if they successfully aided him in claiming the English throne. King William claimed approximately one fifth of land previously held by Kings Harold and Edward. The rest of their territory was divided up amongst William's followers. For instance, he gave Kent to his half-brother Bishop Odo and his boyhood friend William fitzOsbern was given a large amount of land previously owned by King Harold.

King William declared that land belonging to anyone who fought against him at the Battle of Hastings was now his. He confiscated this land under the premise that the previous owners had forfeited it as they had chosen to fight against the rightful King, but this was merely an excuse to legitimise his mass land grab. Again, this territory was given to King William's many followers as a reward for their service.

King William also rewarded his followers financially. Capturing the Royal Treasury at Winchester meant that he had direct access to vast amounts of wealth which he used to reward his men for their service during the invasion. King William also levied heavy taxes on the Anglo-Saxon population which he then used to further reimburse his followers.

William did, however, allow Thegns to buy back their land providing they did not fight against him at Hastings. He also allowed Edwin and Morcar to keep their Earldoms, and in addition to this William also promised to allow the Anglo-Saxon Archbishops Stigand and Aldred to keep their titles and land. This shows he wanted to ensure that the Anglo-Saxons did not feel the need to rebel against him.

Key Points:

- William gave land and money to his followers to reward them for supporting his invasion
- Anglo-Saxon land was confiscated if it was owned by anyone who fought against William at Hasting
- William also gave any wealth he gathered to his followers as a reward for their support
- When King, William raised money from Anglo-Saxons by issuing high taxes
- King William took steps to avoid rebellion by allowing Edwin and Morcar to keep their land in Mercia and Northumbria respectively

The Marcher Earldoms

In addition to avoiding Anglo-Saxon rebellion, King William also took steps to ensure that England was not vulnerable to attacks from neighbouring nations such as Wales. The 'Welsh Marches' or 'Marches' are phrases used to describe the borderlands between England and Wales. Although Wales was not a unified country it did pose numerous problems to Kings of England. Welsh warriors would often raid English territory, stealing goods and livestock in the process. This problem was dealt with by Harold Godwinson when he was an Earl in the 1050s, when he won a military campaign and forced the Welsh Princes to surrender. If King William failed to take steps to deal with Wales he not only risked looking weak in comparison to his predecessor King Harold, but William also risked the possibility of the Welsh allying with Anglo-Saxon rebels.

To effectively deal with this region King William rewarded three of his most trusted followers with land here. Hugh d'Avranches was awarded the earldom of Chester. This, as the northernmost Marcher Earldom, was on the border with north-western Wales. Hugh's father had been one of William's main supporters, providing him with 60 ships for the invasion. Next was the earldom of Shrewsbury which was given to Roger de Montgomery, who had ruled Normandy for William during the invasion of England. Shrewsbury was to the south of Chester. The third and final Marcher Earldom was Hereford and this was given to William fitzOsbern.

As King, William needed to keep the region bordering Wales safe and ensure that it was run efficiently. He therefore gave his Marcher Earls, the men in charge of the three new Marcher Earldoms of Chester, Shrewbury and Hereford, special privileges in comparison to other earls. These included the ability to build castles and churches without the King's permission, direct control of local Sheriffs as well as a non-requirement to pay any form of taxation.

Marcher Earls were extremely powerful and able to act decisively in order to protect the English border with Wales. Their high levels of autonomy meant that they could act quickly and therefore respond to threats effectively. Marcher Earls were, nevertheless, still required to show allegiance to William and were still expected to provide him with military service if called upon.

Key Points:

- To protect the border with Wales William created three new earldoms, called Marcher Earldoms
- Chester, Shrewsbury and Hereford were the names of these new earldoms
- Hugh d'Avranches was awarded the earldom of Chester
- Roger de Montgomery was awarded the earldom of Shrewsbury
- William fitzOsbern was awarded the earldom award of Hereford
- Marcher Earls received special privileges; they did not pay tax, controlled local sheriffs and could build castles or churches without the King's permission
- Marcher Earls helped William establish control as they ensured the border with Wales was secure
- They still had to provide military service to William

The Building of Castles

Marcher Earls were also given the privilege of constructing castles without the King's permission. Castles were extremely important towards William I being able to establish control over England in the years after 1066. The first phase was the building of royal castles. They were often built in strategic locations; William built his first castle when his army invaded in 1066, using it as a staging point from which his army could harass the local Anglo-Saxons, gather resources and ultimately draw Harold Godwinson into battle. The first Norman castles built in England were called Motte and Bailey Castles. Prior to the Norman invasion, the only fortifications found in England were burhs. Motte and bailey castles differed from burhs significantly and for several reasons.

Fortified burhs were designed to be a structure in which a large population of Anglo-Saxons could seek shelter during a Viking Raid, they needed to be large enough to fit the population of a broad geographical area. Motte and bailey castles on the other hand did not need to be large as the Normans were themselves the invader and therefore the minority. A Norman motte and bailey only had to house a small number of soldiers, but it still needed be defensible against a potentially much larger attacking force.

A motte and bailey castle was made up of two parts: the bailey and the motte. The bailey was an enclosed courtyard surrounded by a wall made of wooden stakes known as a palisade. Within the courtyard there were numerous buildings, most often these were halls, kitchens, barracks, stables, workshops, and stores. A bridge connected the bailey to the motte, which was a raised earthwork with a fortified tower, called a keep, on top. Mottes were made from earth and flattened on top. Some mottes were artificial, while others were natural; mounds could be 30 meters high and between 30 to 90 meters in diameter. A ditch often surrounded the motte, with an additional ditch surrounding the perimeter of the bailey and the motte. In the event of an attack the Norman soldiers would flee the bailey and house themselves in the keep on top of the motte until reinforcements arrived. Most motte and bailey castles were 30-40km apart, meaning that if one location was attacked reinforcements could be sent quickly.

As early motte and bailey castles were wooden, they were vulnerable to fire, so over time many of these structures were rebuilt in stone. Norman castles were formidable structures. Initial motte and baileys were quick to construct and served as a reminder to the local Anglo-Saxon population that they were now under the control of William I and his Norman forces. The psychological impact of the building of castles should not be underestimated. These structures acted as a constant reminder of the power and wealth held by the Normans.

William placed castles in important locations such as York, Nottingham and Oxford. Over 500 motte and bailey castles were built by the Normans, some of which are extremely famous. The most famous motte and bailey castle built by William I was Windsor Castle. Windsor Castle was strategically important due to its proximity to the River Thames and Windsor Forest. Following his conquest, William built a defensive ring of castles around London. the ring of castles surrounding London included Windsor Castle, Colchester Castle, Canterbury Castle, Berkhamsted Castle, Guildford Castle, Hertford Castle, Rochester Castle, Oxford Castle, and Wallingford Castle.

However later castles were not constructed by William, but instead by the Norman nobility. They too constructed castles for reasons of strategy, power and control, and, unless they were Marcher Earls, they required royal permission to do so.

Key Points:

- William I built Motte and Bailey Castles to secure his kingdom
- Castles were built in locations of strategic importance such as near towns, river crossings or along important trade routes

- They were small in comparison to burhs as they needed to defend a small number of Normans against potentially large forces of Anglo-Saxon rebels
- The bailey was a courtyard made up of important buildings and surrounded by a wooden palisade
- The motte was a large mound of earth upon which there was a fortified keep
- Soldiers would defend themselves in the keep and wait for reinforcements
- Castles were often 30-40km apart to allow for reinforcements to be sent to any castle under siege
- Castles were also built to act as a reminder of the power and wealth of the Normans – especially when rebuilt in stone
- Over 500 castles were constructed, Windsor Castle was one of many that surrounded London in a protective ring
- Windsor castle was placed strategically close to the River Thames and Windsor Forest
- The first phase was the royal construction of castles. Later phases were led by Norman nobles who also built castles in their Earldoms for reasons of power, strategy or control

2.2 – The Cause and Outcomes of Anglo-Saxon Resistance, 1068–71

The Revolt of Edwin and Morcar, 1068

Despite distributing much of England to his Norman allies, William still had to manage several powerful Anglo-Saxons; Earls Edwin and Morcar were two such individuals. Neither man fought against William at Hastings, electing instead to stay in the North of England in case of another Vikings raid or invasion. Therefore, their land was not forfeit under William's decree that territory owned by the families of those Saxons whom he had battled now belonged to him.

It is likely that both Edwin and Morcar submitted to William at Barking, after he had been crowned King of England. As part of their submission Edwin and Morcar offered William gifts and hostages, and in return they kept their titles and land. Both men were kept at William's court and when he returned to Normandy in 1067 they accompanied him.

During William's absence Bishop Odo and William fitzOsbern were named regents and ruled extremely harshly. There were a number of reported atrocities committed by Norman soldiers and officials against the Anglo-Saxon population. Bishop Odo, who was William's half-brother, was appointed Earl of Kent and given significant power and influence in the south-east of England. According to some accounts, Odo was involved in the brutal suppression of a rebellion in Kent in 1067, during which he ordered the execution of hundreds of rebels and their families. There were also reports that Odo was involved in the widespread confiscation of land and property belonging to Anglo-Saxon nobles, which was then given to his Norman allies. William fitzOsbern, who was appointed Earl of Hereford and tasked with maintaining order in the Welsh borders, was also accused of committing atrocities against the local population. According to some accounts, fitzOsbern ordered the massacre of a group of Welsh hostages who had been taken by his troops, as well as the burning of several villages.

After the Norman Conquest, Edwin and Morcar initially supported William, but they soon became dissatisfied with his rule. They may have felt that they were not being adequately rewarded for their loyalty, or they may have resented the influx of Norman nobles who were given land and power in England. It is believed that Edwin had been promised William's daughter's hand in marriage, but that William eventually went back on this promise. It's worth noting that the exact reasons for Edwin and Morcar's involvement in the revolt are not entirely clear, and historians have debated the issue for centuries. However, it's likely that a combination of factors, including dissatisfaction with William's rule, Norman atrocities committed by William's regents and a desire to maintain their own power and influence played a role in their decision to revolt.

In 1068, Edwin and Morcar joined a revolt against William, along with other Anglo-Saxon nobles. The revolt was centred in the north of England, where there was strong opposition to Norman rule. The rebels besieged York and were initially successful in capturing the city. The Anglo-Saxon force drove out the Norman garrison, but William quickly responded by raising an army and marching north to confront the rebels. The two sides met in battle at the River Aire, where William's forces were able to decisively defeat the rebels.

Edwin and Morcar were forced to submit to William and swear allegiance to him once again. They were not punished severely for their role in the rebellion, however they both lost much of their power and influence in the aftermath of the revolt as William sought to consolidate his control over England and reduce the power of the Anglo-Saxon nobility.

Key Points:

- Edwin and Morcar did not fight against William at the Battle of Hastings so had kept a large proportion of their land
- They submitted to William in 1066
- Edwin and Morcar were kept at William's court as 'guests'
- When William returned to Normandy in 1067 he placed Bishop Odo and William fitzOsbern in charge as his regents
- Each man committed numerous atrocities during their regency
- Many Normans had begun targeting Anglo-Saxons during 1067, taking land and wealth from the population
- Many Anglo-Saxons began to resent Norman rule
- In 1068 Edwin and Morcar escaped William's court and fled north to lead a rebellion
- Edwin was likely frustrated that William had not kept his promise to marry his daughter to Edwin
- Both Edwin and Morcar would have resented the loss of land they had experienced and their declining influence and power in England
- The rebel army captured York and forced the Norman garrison to flee
- William marched an army north and defeated the Anglo-Saxon force at the River Aire
- Edwin and Morcar submitted to William once more and swore allegiance to him
- They were not severely punished but did lose more of their land and power as a consequence

Edgar the Aethling and The Rebellions in the North, 1069

In 1069, there were more rebellions in England against the rule of William. The rebellions were particularly focused in the north of England, where there was still strong opposition to Norman rule. In January of 1069, a rebellion broke out in York, which was quickly followed by uprisings in Durham, Northumberland, and other parts of the north.

The newly appointed Earl of Northumbria, the Norman Robert de Comines, was attacked by Anglo-Saxon forces in Durham during the January of 1069. It is reported by chroniclers that following the defeat of his forces in the streets of Durham, Robert de Comines fled to Bishop Ethelwine's home which was set on fire by the Anglo-Saxon rebels.

Soon after Robert de Comines death, a similar uprising occurred in York which saw the people killing the governor of the town and many Norman troops. Edgar Aethling came down from Scotland and joined the rebels. During the Revolt of Edwin and Morcar in 1068 Edgar the Aethling had been proclaimed as King of England by the Anglo-Saxon rebels. However, before Edgar was able to join the rebellion it had already been defeated by William. Edgar was forced to flee to Scotland for safety. In Scotland, he was given refuge at the court of King Malcolm III and was able to establish himself as a leader of the English exiles who had fled northward to escape Norman rule.

Following the capture of York in 1069, Edgar and the Anglo-Saxon rebel force held out in York castle. Word reached William about what had happened, and he quickly assembled a large army which he marched to York. William forced the rebels out and laid waste to much of the city. Edgar escaped back to Scotland and William built a new castle in York and placed William FitzOsbern in charge. King William left the north and went to Winchester to celebrate Easter.

In autumn of 1069 Edgar the Aethling once more attacked York, this time with the support of King Sweyn of Denmark. The Danish King may have seen an opportunity to take advantage of the instability in England following the Norman Conquest to advance his own interests. King Sweyn may also have had a personal interest in supporting Edgar, who was his kinsman and who had a claim to the English throne. It is also possible that Sweyn was motivated by a desire to avenge the death of his sister, Queen Gunnhild, who had been married to King Harold II of England before the Norman Conquest. Harold had been killed in the Battle of Hastings in 1066, and Sweyn may have seen the rebellion against the Normans as an opportunity to seek revenge.

According to historical accounts, the Anglo-Danish force led by Edgar and Sweyn launched a surprise attack on the York, catching the Norman garrison off guard. They were able to breach the walls of the city and engage in fierce fighting with the Normans, who ultimately proved to be outnumbered and outmatched. The Anglo-Danish force was able to seize control of the city and establish a base of operations from which they could launch further attacks against Norman forces in the region. Following the capture of the city, much of York's wealth was seized by the Danish forces and stored on their fleet of ships.

William, who was in the south of England at the time, immediately raised an army and marched north to confront the rebels. He arrived in York in December 1069 and began a siege of the city, which lasted for several weeks. During the siege, William's army engaged in a scorched-earth policy, destroying crops, burning villages, and slaughtering livestock in the surrounding countryside. This made it difficult for the rebels to obtain food and supplies and weakened their position. After several weeks of siege, the Anglo-Danish army attempted to break out of the city and engage the Norman army in open battle. However, they were quickly defeated by the Normans, who were better equipped and more experienced in battle. The Normans pursued the rebels, killing many of them and driving the rest into the wilderness. The Anglo-Danish invasion had failed, and the rebellion against Norman rule was gradually suppressed over the following year.

William's victory at the Battle of York in 1069 was a significant turning point in the Norman Conquest of England, as it demonstrated the Norman army's strength and resilience in the face of a major rebellion.

The victory also allowed William to consolidate his control over northern England and put an end to the threat of further Anglo-Danish invasions.

Key Points:

- In 1069 there were more rebellions in the north of England
- Robert de Comines, the Norman Earl of Northumbria, was killed by Anglo-Saxon rebels in Durham during the January of 1069
- Edgar Aethling led a separate Anglo-Saxon force which captured York, but this was defeated by William and Edgar fled back to Scotland
- In autumn of 1069 Edgar Aethling once more led an Anglo-Saxon attack on York, this time with the support of King Sweyn of Denmark
- The surprise attack resulted in the defeat of the Norman forces controlling York
- William once again marched north to defeat the rebel force and besieged York
- He starved the city of supplies by ordering his forces to destroy the areas surrounding York
- William was eventually able to defeat the Anglo-Danish force during the Battle of York, when, running low on supplies, the armies of Edgar and Sweyn attempted to break out of the city
- This was unsuccessful and William was able to defeat the rebellion

Hereward the Wake and Rebellion at Ely, 1070–71

Hereward the Wake was an Anglo-Saxon. At the age of around eighteen it is believed that he was exiled from England due to disobedience to his father and general disruption which led to problems in his local community. Hereward was declared an outlaw by Edward the Confessor and is believed to have spent most of his time fighting in conflicts in Europe, mainly in Flanders.

When William invaded England in 1066 Hereward the Wake was still in Flanders, fighting as a mercenary for Count Baldwin V of Flanders. He probably arrived back in England in 1067 or 1068. Upon his return to England Hereward discovered that the Normans had seized his family's lands and murdered his brother. In response to this Hereward kills fifteen Normans, including local nobles who had taken his family lands. Soon afterwards, he journeyed to Peterborough Abbey where he was knighted by his uncle and then briefly returned to the continent where he spent time in Flanders, planning his next move.

The story of Hereward the Wake is covered in numerous chronicles and historical accounts, some of which are clearly exaggerative in comparison to others. It is using the more realistic of these accounts that it is possible to construct a narrative of Hereward the Wake and the rebellion at Ely in the years 1070 to 1071. In 1070 another Danish fleet sailed to England. As a result of his exploits, Hereward had amassed numerous supporters due to his celebrity status and it is this force that greeted the Danish on the Isle of Ely. By this point Hereward's uncle had been replaced as the Abbot of Peterborough Abbey, so Hereward and the Danish launched a raid on this site and robbed it of all its riches.

Upon their return to the Isle of Ely the combined force of Hereward and the Danes was joined by an Anglo-Saxon army led by Earl Morcar. The Danes, however, did not remain for long and instead returned to Denmark with the wealth they had gathered from the raid on Peterborough Abbey.

William gathered a force and set his sights on defeating the combined forces of Hereward and Morcar, surrounding the Isle of Ely in 1071. The Isle of Ely was an island surrounded by a large area of fenland, a type of swamp, which was very easy to defend.

Following a prolonged struggle, William was able to defeat the force garrisoned on the Isle. He did this by bribing local monks who were able to provide him with details of a route onto the Isle at low tide. Using this pathway William's forces stormed the area; unable to detain Hereward and his band of men who subsequently evaded capture by escaping across the fenlands, William was able to capture Morcar who was subsequently imprisoned in Normandy for the remainder of his life.

Key Points:

- Hereward the Wake was exiled from England when he was eighteen years old
- He spent several years fighting abroad as a mercenary
- During the conquest of 1066, Hereward was fighting for the Count of Flanders in mainland Europe
- Hereward returned to England in 1067 or 1068 to find his family had been murdered by Normans and that their lands had been seized
- In response to this, Hereward killed fifteen Normans before returning to Flanders
- Hereward returned to England in 1070 and joined forces with a Danish fleet
- This combined force sacked Peterborough Abbey and the Danish fleet returned to Denmark with the abbey's wealth
- William was eventually able to defeat the rebel force

2.3 – The legacy of resistance to 1087

The Harrying of the North

As previously covered, once he was crowned king in 1066 William faced multiple instances of resistance to his rule. In 1068 and 1069 there were three significant threats in the north of England, each of which were swiftly dealt with by William. By medieval standards, William's response to the revolt led by Edwin and Morcar in 1068 was fairly measured. Likewise, when another rebellion commenced in the first half of 1069 William's response was again reasonable. Yet despite William's considerably fair approach to these instances of Anglo-Saxon resistance he once again faced resistance in the north later in 1069. By now William's patience had grown thin and he no doubt felt as though the Anglo-Saxons in the north required a firmer hand. What followed has come to be referred to as 'The Harrying of the North'.

William ordered the Harrying of the North for several reasons. One of the main reasons was to crush the rebellion that had broken out in the north of England in 1069. In addition to quashing the rebellion, William also wanted to make an example of the North; William saw the North as a potential source of future rebellion and unrest, and he wanted to send a message that resistance to Norman rule would not be tolerated. Another factor was the attacks on Norman garrisons and castles that had taken place during the rebellion. William saw these attacks as a direct challenge to his authority and felt that he needed to respond in a forceful and decisive manner. By laying waste to the North, he hoped to demonstrate his power and deter any further acts of resistance. Finally, there was an economic motive behind the Harrying of the North. The region was known for its fertile farmland and prosperous towns, and William's army seized vast amounts of livestock and crops during the campaign. This helped to feed his troops and replenish his resources, while also denying these resources to the rebels.

The campaign began in late 1069. William's army, led by his half-brother Odo and other Norman commanders, embarked on a scorched-earth campaign of destruction, burning villages, crops, and livestock. The goal was to deny the rebels any resources that could sustain them and to break the will of the Northumbrian people. The army moved methodically across the region, devastating the countryside and massacring anyone who resisted. According to some accounts, the death toll may have reached as high as 100,000 people, though the exact number is impossible to determine. Survivors of the campaign were forced to flee their homes and seek refuge elsewhere, often facing starvation and disease on the way. William's army also engaged in a systematic campaign of land confiscation, seizing vast tracts of territory from the Northumbrian nobles who had rebelled against him and redistributing them to Norman followers. This helped to consolidate Norman control over the region and further marginalise the Anglo-Saxon population.

The campaign left a trail of devastation across the North, with villages burned to the ground, crops destroyed, and livestock slaughtered. Tens of thousands of people died because of the campaign, either through direct violence or from starvation and disease. Survivors of the campaign were forced to flee their homes and seek refuge elsewhere. Many went to other parts of England, while others fled to Scotland or Scandinavia. This led to a significant displacement of people and a disruption of the social fabric of the region. The Normans seized vast tracts of land from the Northumbrian nobles who had rebelled against him and distributed them to his Norman followers. This helped to solidify Norman control over the region and marginalise the Anglo-Saxon population. The Harrying of the North had a lasting impact on the North of England, both in terms of its physical landscape and its cultural identity. Many towns and villages were never rebuilt, and the region remained economically and culturally marginalised for centuries to come. The campaign became part of the historical memory of the North, serving as a symbol of resistance to outside rule and a source of regional pride. This memory was passed down through generations and helped to shape the region's identity and culture.

Key Points:

- William faced multiple instances of resistance in the north of England in 1068 and 1069
- His responses to early revolts were relatively measured
- Frustration led to the Harrying of the North in late 1069
- Goals of the campaign:
  - Crush the northern rebellion
  - Make an example of the North to deter future resistance
  - Respond to attacks on Norman garrisons and castles
  - Seize resources to feed William's army and deny them to rebels
- It was a scorched-earth campaign led by William's half-brother Odo and other Norman commanders
- The death toll potentially reached 100,000, with survivors facing starvation and disease
- Norman land confiscation helped consolidate control over the region
- Lasting impact on the North of England:
  - Devastation of landscape and villages
  - Displacement of people
  - Disruption of social fabric
  - Economic and cultural marginalisation
  - Served as a symbol of resistance and source of regional pride for centuries

Changes in Landownership

The changes in landownership from Anglo-Saxon to Norman during the years 1066–1087 were profound and shaped the future of England. This period saw the decline of Anglo-Saxon nobility and the rise of the Normans, who took control of the land and instituted a new social and political order.

Following the Battle of Hastings, William confiscated the lands and properties of the Anglo-Saxon nobles who had opposed him. This allowed him to weaken the power of the Anglo-Saxon nobility and reward his Norman followers for their loyalty and support during the invasion. Many Anglo-Saxon nobles lost their lands and titles, and some were even forced into exile. After confiscating the lands of the Anglo-Saxon nobility, William redistributed these lands among his Norman followers who then became the new ruling class in England. This helped to establish a loyal base of support among the new Norman aristocracy, who were now indebted to William for their newfound wealth and power.

These land-grabs were a crucial part of the Norman strategy for controlling England after the conquest. By redistributing land amongst his own followers, William ensured that the new ruling class was loyal to him, and by implementing the feudal system, they were able to maintain centralised control over the land and resources of the kingdom. Under this system, the king granted land to his tenants-in-chief, who in turn granted lands to their own vassals. This hierarchical structure replaced the more decentralised Anglo-Saxon system and helped consolidate Norman control over the land.

Based on the Domesday Book and other historical records, it is estimated that by 1086, approximately 90% of the land in England was owned by Normans and other foreigners. Before the conquest, the Anglo-Saxon nobility held much of this land. The redistribution of land and resources was a key element of William's strategy to consolidate his rule and reward his Norman followers. The number of Anglo-Saxon thegns (nobles) fell from around 4,000 before the Conquest to fewer than 200 by

1086. Many lost their lands and titles, while others were forced into exile. The number of tenants-in-chief, who held land directly from the king, was around 180 in 1086. Of these, only two were Anglo-Saxons, with the majority being Normans or other foreigners. William granted large tracts of land to a select group of Norman nobles, who became some of the most powerful landholders in England. For example, the Earl of Surrey, William de Warenne, received lands in 13 different counties. The Norman Church also benefited from the redistribution of land, with the Archbishop of Canterbury, Lanfranc, himself a Norman, receiving extensive landholdings throughout England.

These figures illustrate the scale of the shift in landownership from the Anglo-Saxons to the Normans following the Conquest. The redistribution of land played a crucial role in establishing a new social and political order in England, consolidating the power of the Normans and their allies.

Key Points:

- There were profound changes in landownership from Anglo-Saxons to Normans during the period 1066-1087
- The decline of the Anglo-Saxon nobility coincided with the rise of the Normans
- Post-Battle of Hastings there was a confiscation and redistribution of lands from Anglo-Saxon nobles to Norman followers
- Norman followers became new ruling class
- Redistribution of land was crucial for William's control strategy
- By 1086, around 90% of land in England owned by Normans and foreigners
- The was a significant decline in the number of Anglo-Saxon thegns
- Tenants-in-chief were now mostly Normans and foreigners
- Large tracts of land were granted to select Norman nobles
- The Norman Church benefited from land redistribution

Maintaining Royal Power

Once he was crowned king in 1066, it was important for William to maintain royal power for several reasons. William's claim to the English throne was contested, as he was a foreign ruler from Normandy, and some English nobles considered his rule to be illegitimate. By maintaining and consolidating his power, William could secure his position and assert his authority as the rightful king. Furthermore, the period leading up to William's reign was marked by political turmoil, with multiple contenders vying for the English throne.

Maintaining strong royal power was necessary for providing stability and order to a fractured kingdom. To effectively govern this kingdom, William needed to assert control over the Anglo-Saxon nobility, who during his early reign still held significant power and influence. By maintaining strong royal authority, William could reduce the risk of rebellion and ensure that his rule was respected. England also faced potential threats from neighbouring kingdoms and hostile factions; maintaining a strong grip on power meant that William could safeguard the kingdom against both internal and external threats. Lastly, as a Norman ruler, William sought to integrate his own culture and customs into English society. By maintaining strong royal power, he could more effectively promote the fusion of Norman and Anglo-Saxon traditions, which would ultimately help to forge a unified and cohesive English identity.

William employed numerous methods to assist him in maintaining his power. Perhaps the most well known is his introduction of the feudal system in England; under this system, land was distributed to his loyal followers in exchange for military service and loyalty, and by doing so, he effectively established a hierarchy where everyone owed allegiance to him. Another equally well-known method is the Domesday Book. In 1086, William ordered a comprehensive survey of his newly acquired kingdom, known as the Domesday Book. This survey listed all landowners, their properties, and the resources they controlled. The primary purpose of the book was to assess taxes, but it also helped William to keep track of who owned what land, making it harder for potential rebellions to gain support and resources.

William built numerous castles and fortifications across England, such as the Tower of London and Windsor Castle. These structures served as symbols of his power and authority, demonstrating his control over the land. They also provided him with strategic military outposts to suppress rebellions and protect his territory from external threats. William also replaced much of the Anglo-Saxon nobility with his own Norman followers. This helped him establish control over the local population and eliminate potential rivals. By surrounding himself with loyal Norman nobles, William ensured that he had a trusted network of supporters who would help him maintain his rule.

To maintain his power, William required the nobility and clergy to swear an oath of loyalty to him. This made it clear that they were his subjects, and any refusal to swear allegiance could be seen as an act of treason, punishable by death or confiscation of property. William maintained a close relationship with the Church, using it to legitimize his rule. He appointed loyal bishops and abbots, ensuring that they would support him politically. Additionally, he made substantial donations to monastic communities, which further solidified his relationship with the Church and reinforced his image as a pious and God-fearing ruler.

William and his followers also imposed the Norman language and culture on the English population. This created a cultural divide between the ruling Normans and the native English, making it more difficult for the English to unite against their new rulers. The use of the French language in official documents and court proceedings also solidified the position of the Normans as the ruling class.

In summary, William I maintained royal power after 1066 through a combination of strategic military and political actions, as well as cultural impositions. By implementing the feudal system, building castles, replacing Anglo-Saxon nobility, and leveraging the Church's authority, he was able to secure his rule over England for years to come.

Key Points:

- William's contested claim to the throne required strong royal power
- He asserted his control over Anglo-Saxon nobility to reduce the risk of rebellion
- William promoted a fusion of Norman and Anglo-Saxon traditions
- He introduced the feudal system to establish a hierarchy and ensure loyalty
- Castles were built as symbols of power and strategic military outposts
- William replaced the Anglo-Saxon nobility with Norman followers
- All nobility and clergy had to swear an oath of loyalty

2.4 – The Revolt of the Earls, 1075

Reasons for the Revolt

Although 1071 is seen as the last Anglo-Saxon revolt against William's rule, he still faced resistance in 1075 from his Norman Tenants-in-Chief. This revolt was largely a consequence of the earls' dissatisfaction with William's rule and policies.

The leaders of the Revolt of the Earls in 1075 were three powerful English earls. Waltheof, Earl of Northumbria, was the most prominent of the rebel leaders and was highly respected by the English people. Although an Anglo-Saxon, Waltheof's involvement was but one-third of the revolt and thus this is not regarded as being a form of Anglo-Saxon resistance. Roger de Breteuil, Earl of Hereford, was a Norman noble who had been granted extensive estates in England by William. However, he joined the rebellion due to his opposition to William's appointment of foreign bishops and other policies. Ralph de Gael, Earl of East Anglia, was a Breton noble who had been granted estates in East Anglia by William. Ralph also joined the rebellion due to his dissatisfaction with William's rule. These three earls were also joined by several other English nobles who shared their grievances against William. Together, they sought to challenge William's authority and policies, but ultimately failed to overthrow him.

One of the major factors that led to the revolt was William's appointment of foreign bishops to English dioceses. This was seen as an infringement on the traditional rights of the English nobility to appoint clerics to positions within their own estates. The earls were also unhappy with William's heavy taxation and his imposition of a new system of forest laws, which restricted their hunting rights and use of forest lands. Land also played a significant role; Roger felt aggrieved that his earldom had reduced in size, whilst Waltheof and Ralph must also have held concerns that their land would be reduced in size. Furthermore, the earls were also frustrated by William's use of sheriffs, as they felt that this undermined their own authority in their earldoms.

The specific plan for the Revolt of the Earls in 1075 is not well-documented in historical records. The general aim of the rebellion was to challenge the authority of King William I and to seek greater autonomy and influence for the English nobility. It is likely that the earls planned to use their combined military strength and influence to challenge William's authority and force him to negotiate new terms of governance that would be more favourable to the English nobility.

Key Points:

- In 1075, William faced resistance from his Norman Tenants-in-Chief due to dissatisfaction with his rule and policies.
- The leaders of the Revolt of the Earls in 1075 were three powerful earls: Waltheof of Northumbria, Roger de Breteuil of Hereford, and Ralph de Gael of East Anglia.
- They were joined by several other English nobles who shared their grievances against William.
- The revolt was caused by William's appointment of foreign bishops, heavy taxation, imposition of forest laws, land disputes, and the use of sheriffs.
- The aim of the revolt was to challenge William's authority and seek greater autonomy for the English nobility. The specific plan for the revolt is not well-documented, but the earls likely planned to use their military strength to force William to negotiate new terms of governance.

The Defeat of the Revolt

Lanfranc, the Archbishop of Canterbury during the time of the Revolt of the Earls in 1075, played a significant role in the events surrounding the rebellion. As William was in Normandy during the early stages of the revolt, Lanfranc was acting as regent on his behalf.

It was Lanfranc who attempted to mediate between the rebellious earls and the king. He urged them to abandon the revolt and seek reconciliation with William, however his efforts were ultimately unsuccessful, as the earls persisted in their rebellion. As the Archbishop of Canterbury, Lanfranc held significant religious authority and played a crucial role in legitimising William's rule. He provided religious justification and support for the king's policies and actions, including suppressing the revolt. Lanfranc likely had a role in issuing excommunications against the rebel leaders, thereby condemning their actions as rebellious and undermining their religious standing within the Catholic Church. This would have further weakened their support and legitimacy.

Waltheof, the Earl of Northumbria and one of the main rebel leaders, changed sides and provided valuable information to King William. His betrayal likely played a significant role in the suppression of the revolt. It is believed that it was Waltheof who informed Lanfranc of the revolt, a betrayal which enabled the regent to take the necessary actions to suppress the revolt.

Royal forces were swiftly gathered, and Roger was unable to exit his earldom to join forces with Ralph, who's earldom was on the other side of the country. Roger was besieged in Hereford castle, isolating the rebels within and placing extreme pressure on Roger and his forces. By successfully besieging Hereford Castle, William effectively neutralised one of the key leaders of the revolt.

Ralph was dealt with in a similar manner. He too was prevented from exiting his earldom of East Anglia and decided to take refuge in Norwich Castle. Royal forces initiated a siege, cutting off supplies and isolating the rebels within the castle. Ralph did not receive the expected support from other rebel forces, and he found himself isolated in his resistance. Without sufficient reinforcements or aid, his position within the castle became increasingly precarious.

After Waltheof betrayed the revolt and provided information to King William, Lanfranc played a role in attempting to reconcile him with the king. Despite his cooperation, Waltheof was captured by William's forces, taken into custody and imprisoned - likely to prevent any potential future rebellion or to keep him under control. Waltheof's fate was ultimately sealed through a trial for treason. In 1076, he was brought before a court and accused of participating in the revolt against William. Despite his cooperation and previous loyalty to the king, Waltheof was found guilty of treason and sentenced to death. In May 1076, Waltheof was executed by beheading. His execution took place at St. Giles's Hill near Winchester, and it is reported that he faced his death with courage and dignity. His execution marked the only case of an English noble being executed by William's orders. The execution of Waltheof sent a powerful message about William's determination to maintain his authority and quell any form of rebellion, even from those who had previously shown loyalty.

Regarding what happened to Roger after the revolt, historical records provide limited details. However, it is believed that Roger was captured by William's forces after the suppression of the rebellion. As for his fate, it is believed that Roger faced severe consequences for his involvement in the revolt. He likely lost his lands and titles, and it is possible that he was imprisoned or exiled. Unfortunately, the specific details of his punishment or later life are not clearly recorded.

Following the suppression of the revolt, Ralph was captured by, although the details of his capture are not extensively documented. As a rebel leader, Ralph faced severe repercussions for his actions. He was stripped of his lands and titles, effectively losing his position as Earl of East Anglia. The extent of his punishment beyond the loss of his earldom is not specifically recorded. It is believed that Ralph was subsequently exiled from England because of his involvement in the revolt. He likely had to leave the country and seek refuge elsewhere, unable to return or regain his former status. The historical records are sparse when it comes to Ralph's fate and later life. There is limited information about his activities or whereabouts following his exile, thus the details of his eventual demise are not well-documented.

Key Points:

- Lanfranc, acting as regent for King William I, attempted to mediate between the rebellious earls and the king, but his efforts to convince them to abandon the revolt were unsuccessful
- As the Archbishop of Canterbury, Lanfranc played a crucial role in legitimising William's rule and provided religious support for the king's actions, including suppressing the revolt
- Lanfranc likely issued excommunications against the rebel leaders, weakening their support and legitimacy within the Catholic Church
- Waltheof, one of the rebel leaders, changed sides and provided valuable information to King William, which played a significant role in suppressing the revolt
- Roger de Breteuil was besieged in Hereford Castle, and Ralph de Gael sought refuge in Norwich Castle, isolating them and placing pressure on their forces
- After the revolt, Waltheof was captured, imprisoned, and brought to trial for treason. He was found guilty and executed by beheading
- Details about Roger de Breteuil's punishment or later life are limited, but he likely lost his lands and titles, and may have been imprisoned or exiled
- Ralph de Gael was stripped of his lands and titles, exiled from England, and his fate and later life are not well-documented in historical records

Key Topic 3 – Norman England, 1066-1088

This key topic focuses upon the ways in which England changed under Norman control.

3.1 – The Feudal System and The Church

Feudal Hierarchy and Feudalism

Feudalism was a social, economic, and political system that was prevalent during the Middle Ages throughout Europe, including Norman England. The feudal hierarchy in Norman England consisted of several levels, with the king at the top, followed by tenants-in-chief, knights, and peasants.

At the top of the feudal hierarchy was the king, who held ultimate authority over the land and its people. He granted land to his tenants-in-chief in exchange for their loyalty, military support, and tax revenue. Tenants-in-chief were powerful nobles who held large tracts of land directly from the king. In exchange for this land, they pledged their loyalty and provided military support to the king, often by supplying knights for his army. Knights were professional soldiers who held smaller portions of land from the tenants-in-chief, in exchange for providing military service. They were expected to fight for their lord in times of war and maintain law and order within their territories. As they held tracts of land from the Tenants-in-chief they are also referred to as Under-tenants.

At the bottom of the hierarchy were the Anglo-Saxon peasants, who worked the land and provided labour and resources for their lords. The Norman feudal hierarchy played a significant role in suppressing the Anglo-Saxons after the Norman Conquest. As William sought to consolidate his power and secure his rule, he implemented various strategies within the feudal system to suppress the native Saxon population. One of the most significant ways the feudal hierarchy suppressed the Anglo-Saxons was through the confiscation of land from Saxon nobles and its redistribution to Norman nobles and knights. By replacing the Anglo-Saxon aristocracy with Norman tenants-in-chief and knights, William effectively eliminated the power base of the native Saxon nobility and ensured the loyalty of his new Norman vassals.

The Normans introduced new laws, customs, and administrative practices that replaced the existing Anglo-Saxon system. This included the imposition of the Norman feudal hierarchy, which further marginalised the Anglo-Saxon population by placing them under the control of the new Norman lords. The Anglo-Saxons were pressured into adopting the Normans' language, culture, and customs. Use of the English language was discouraged in favour of Norman French, particularly among the upper classes, which further marginalised the native population.

Feudalism was characterised by a system of land tenure, where land was held by vassals from their lords in exchange for various services. This created a network of mutual obligations and responsibilities, binding the members of society together. In Norman England, the primary focus was on military service and loyalty to the king. Land was the primary source of wealth and power in feudal society. It was divided into estates or manors, which were managed by a lord or his representative. The lord would grant land to his vassals in return for their loyalty and services, creating a complex web of relationships and obligations. Knight service was a key component of feudalism in Norman England. Knights were professional soldiers who were granted land by their lords in exchange for military service. They were expected to maintain a certain number of horses, armour, and weapons and be ready to fight for their lord when called upon. Peasants, who made up the majority of the population, were required to provide labour services to their lords. This typically involved working on the lord's lands, maintaining roads and bridges, or providing other forms of labour as needed. In exchange, they were allowed to farm small plots of land for their own use and were protected by their lord.

If a vassal failed to fulfil his obligations to his lord, such as providing military service or paying taxes, he could face forfeiture; the vassal's land would be confiscated and redistributed to another vassal who was loyal to the lord. This served as a powerful incentive for vassals to remain loyal and fulfil their responsibilities.

Homage was a crucial aspect of the feudal system in Norman England, as it served to formalise the relationship between a lord and his vassal. When a vassal received land from his lord, they were required to pay homage, which was a public ceremony where the vassal pledged loyalty and fidelity to their lord. During the ceremony of homage, the vassal would kneel before the lord and place his hands between those of the lord, symbolising submission and the acceptance of the lord's authority. The vassal would then swear an oath of fealty, pledging to remain loyal and defend his lord against all enemies. In return, the lord would promise to protect the vassal and uphold his rights. Homage served to strengthen the bond between the lord and vassal, creating a sense of loyalty and obligation that was crucial to maintaining the stability of the feudal system. By pledging their loyalty and military support, vassals ensured that their lords would continue to protect them and their lands, thereby maintaining the hierarchy and order of feudal society. The act of homage was not limited to the relationship between the king and his tenants-in-chief. Knights also paid homage to their lords (the tenants-in-chief) and were bound by the same oaths of loyalty and fidelity. This created a hierarchical chain of loyalty that extended from the king down to the lowest levels of society, reinforcing the structure of the feudal system and the social order of Norman England.

Feudalism in Norman England from 1066 to 1088 was a complex system of land tenure, social hierarchy, and mutual obligations. The king held ultimate authority and granted land to his tenants-in-chief, who in turn granted land to knights in exchange for military service. Peasants provided labour services to their lords and could farm small plots of land for their own use. The entire system was held together by a network of loyalties and obligations, ensuring stability and order in a turbulent time.

Key Points:

- The feudal hierarchy in Norman England had the king at the top, followed by tenants-in-chief, knights, and peasants.
- The king granted land to tenants-in-chief in exchange for loyalty, military support, and taxes.
- Tenants-in-chief held land from the king, pledged loyalty, and provided military support.
- Knights, as professional soldiers, held land from tenants-in-chief and provided military service.
- Anglo-Saxon peasants worked the land and provided resources for their lords.
- The Norman feudal hierarchy suppressed the Anglo-Saxons through land confiscation and redistribution which favoured the Normans.
- The Normans replaced Anglo-Saxon laws and customs, imposing a new hierarchy, and marginalising the native population.
- Feudalism focused on land tenure and mutual obligations, with an emphasis on military service and loyalty.
- Knight service and peasant labour service were essential components of feudalism in Norman England.
- Forfeiture could occur if a vassal failed to fulfil obligations to their lord.
- Homage ceremonies formalised relationships between lords and vassals, reinforcing loyalty and the feudal hierarchy.

The Church in Norman England

The Church in England between 1066 and 1088 experienced significant changes. This period saw the rise of Norman influence and the reform of the Church, which had lasting effects on society, government, and religious life in England. Key figures such as Stigand and Lanfranc played crucial roles in this transformation.

Before the Norman Conquest in 1066, the Church in England was a loosely organised institution with significant regional variations. The role of the Church in society was primarily focused on providing spiritual guidance and services to the population, while its relationship with the government was relatively informal. The Norman Conquest brought significant changes to the Church in England. William sought to use the Church to consolidate and maintain control over the newly conquered lands.

Stigand, the Archbishop of Canterbury, was an important figure during the early period of Norman rule. He maintained a close relationship with the English nobility and the ruling class. However, his questionable appointment as Archbishop and his refusal to support the papal-backed Norman invasion led to his eventual excommunication and removal from office. One of the main accusations against Stigand was his involvement in simony, which is the practice of buying or selling ecclesiastical offices or positions. It is believed that Stigand purchased his appointment to the archbishopric of Canterbury, which was a blatant violation of Church law. Stigand was also accused of pluralism, as he held multiple high-ranking ecclesiastical positions simultaneously. He was not only the Archbishop of Canterbury but also retained his position as the Bishop of Winchester. Holding multiple offices was considered a form of corruption, as it indicated a desire for wealth and power rather than genuine spiritual leadership. Furthermore, Stigand's appointment as the Archbishop of Canterbury was never formally approved by the Pope. His predecessor, Archbishop Robert of Jumièges, had been deposed by King Edward the Confessor, and Stigand was appointed in his place without seeking papal consent. This irregular appointment cast doubt on Stigand's legitimacy and contributed to his reputation as a corrupt figure. Stigand was known for his close ties to the English nobility, including King Harold Godwinson, an association which led some to believe that Stigand was more interested in furthering his own political ambitions rather than in serving the Church. His refusal to support the papal-backed Norman invasion, which led to the Battle of Hastings in 1066, further fuelled suspicions of corruption. All these factors combined to create a perception of Stigand as a corrupt figure within the Church. His eventual excommunication and removal from office by the Normans under William's rule served to reinforce this view.

Lanfranc, a highly respected scholar and prior of the Abbey of Bec in Normandy, was appointed Archbishop of Canterbury by William I in 1070. He played a crucial role in the Normanisation and reform of the Church in England. Under his guidance, the Church became more closely aligned with the Roman Catholic Church, adopting many of its practices and principles. Under Lanfranc's leadership, the Church underwent significant changes, both in its organisation and in its relationship with the government. One of the major reforms was the introduction of a more hierarchical structure, with the archbishops and bishops exercising greater control over the lower clergy. This helped to establish a more unified and efficient Church, which was essential for the implementation of William's policies. The Church also became more closely tied to the government under Norman rule. Bishops and abbots were often appointed from among the Norman aristocracy, ensuring loyalty to the king. Moreover, the Church played an important role in the administration and collection of taxes, as well as in the establishment and maintenance of law and order.

The Church was an essential tool for William to maintain control over England. The close relationship between the Church and the government allowed him to use its resources and influence to assert his authority. The Church also provided a crucial means of communication and control, allowing William to disseminate his policies and maintain law and order throughout the kingdom.

The transformation of the Church in England had a significant impact on the lives of the people. The adoption of Roman Catholic practices and principles led to a more uniform and standardised religious experience for the population. The construction of new churches, monasteries, and cathedrals also contributed to a greater emphasis on religion in daily life. The increased influence of the Norman aristocracy on the Church also brought about changes in the social and cultural life of England. The new elite introduced Norman customs and traditions, including new styles of architecture, art, and literature. The Church played a crucial role in promoting and disseminating these new cultural influences throughout the country.

Under Norman rule, The Church placed greater emphasis on education, particularly within monastic institutions. This led to the establishment of new schools and the promotion of literacy, especially among the clergy. As a result, the intellectual landscape of England underwent a significant transformation, with Latin becoming the dominant language of scholarship and administration. The close relationship between the Church and the government under William had an impact on the development of law and governance in England. The Church also played a crucial role in the administration of justice, with bishops and other high-ranking clergy often serving as judges in ecclesiastical courts. Furthermore, the Church contributed to the codification of laws and the development of legal principles that would shape the English legal system for centuries to come.

The Church in England between 1066 and 1088 underwent a profound transformation, particularly during the reign of William I. The Normanisation and reform of the Church not only changed its structure and relationship with the government but also had a lasting impact on the social, cultural, and intellectual life of the country. Key figures such as Stigand and Lanfranc played pivotal roles in this process, and the Church emerged as a central institution in maintaining control and shaping the development of England under Norman rule.

Key Points:

- Before the Norman Conquest, the Church was loosely organised and had an informal relationship with the government.
- William sought to use the Church to consolidate and maintain control over the newly conquered lands.
- Stigand, the Archbishop of Canterbury, faced accusations of corruption, including simony, pluralism, and having close ties to the English nobility.
- Lanfranc, appointed by William I as Archbishop of Canterbury, helped in the Normanisation and reform of the Church in England, aligning it more closely with the Roman Catholic Church.
- The Church's organisational structure and relationship with the government underwent significant changes under William I.
- The Church played a crucial role in maintaining control over England, serving as a means of communication and control.
- The transformation of the Church in England impacted religious, social, cultural, and intellectual life, as well as law and governance in the country.

Changes to Anglo Saxon Society and Economy

During the period 410-1066, Anglo-Saxon England witnessed significant political, social, and economic changes as it transformed from a group of disparate Germanic tribes to a unified kingdom under the rule of the House of Wessex. The Norman Conquest in 1066 marked another major turning point in English history, introducing a new ruling elite and initiating changes in governance, landholding, and social customs.

The Anglo-Saxon society was characterised by a hierarchical social structure, with the king at the top, followed by the nobility, free peasants, and slaves. The Norman Conquest led to a significant reshuffling of the social order, as the new Norman rulers replaced the native Anglo-Saxon aristocracy. Many Anglo-Saxon nobles were dispossessed of their lands, which were granted to Norman lords loyal to William. This redistribution of land created a new upper class composed primarily of Normans and altered the existing power dynamics.

The Norman Conquest also had a profound impact on language and culture in England. The Normans spoke a variety of Old French known as Anglo-Norman, which influenced the development of the English language. Many Old English words were replaced or adapted with Norman French equivalents, leading to a more diverse vocabulary. Additionally, the Normans introduced new cultural practices, such as chivalry, which influenced the way the Anglo-Saxon society functioned.

The Anglo-Saxon legal system was characterised by a combination of customary laws and royal decrees. The Norman Conquest introduced new administrative practices, including the establishment of centralised royal authority and the creation of new legal institutions. One such innovation was the Domesday Book, a comprehensive survey of landholdings and resources throughout England, which served as a basis for taxation and governance.

The Anglo-Saxon economy was predominantly agrarian, with much of the population engaged in subsistence farming. The introduction of the three-field crop rotation system during the late Anglo-Saxon period led to an increase in agricultural productivity, which, in turn, contributed to population growth. The Normans continued to develop the agricultural sector, introducing new techniques and expanding the use of arable land. Trade played a crucial role in the Anglo-Saxon economy, particularly in the later period. The growth of towns and the establishment of trade routes facilitated the exchange of goods both domestically and internationally. The Normans further fostered trade by building new towns, such as the port of Liverpool, and establishing new trade connections with continental Europe. This was a shift from the Anglo-Saxon period, during which trade was much more common with Scandinavia.

Craftsmanship and industry were integral components of the Anglo-Saxon economy. Skilled craftsmen produced a variety of goods, including textiles, pottery, and metalwork. The growth of towns during the late Anglo-Saxon period led to an increase in specialised production, as craftsmen began to cluster in urban centres. The Norman Conquest did not drastically alter the nature of craftsmanship and industry in England; however, it did introduce new forms of artistic expression and architectural styles.

As a result of the Norman Conquest England experienced significant social and economic change. The transformation of the social hierarchy, the impact on language and culture, and the changes in law and administration demonstrate the far-reaching effects of the Conquest. At the same time, the Anglo-Saxon economy experienced growth and diversification in areas such as agriculture, trade, and craftsmanship, which continued to evolve under Norman rule. While the Conquest brought about significant upheaval and change, it also facilitated the development of a more complex and interconnected society, laying the foundations for the emergence of a distinctive English identity in the centuries that followed.

Key Points:

- The Norman conquest marked a major turning point in English History
- As a result of the Norman Conquest there was a reshuffling of the social order, with Normans replacing Anglo-Saxons as the social elite
- Many Old English words were replaced by or adapted with Norman French words
- The Norman Conquest led to the English language becoming much more diverse
- Numerous economic changes occurred as a result of the Norman Conquest, particularly trade, as trade connections with mainland Europe improved
- Trade focus shifted from Scandinavia towards Normandy and France

3.2 – Norman Government

Changes After the Conquest

William introduced a range of reforms aimed at consolidating his power and maintaining control over the newly conquered territory. One of the most significant changes introduced by William I was the centralisation of power in the hands of the king. Prior to the Conquest, the Anglo-Saxon government operated under a decentralised system, with power dispersed among various regional authorities. However, after 1066, William sought to establish a more unified and efficient system of governance, with the monarchy at the helm.

To achieve this, William introduced a series of reforms. The dispossessing of Anglo-Saxon nobles and the redistribution of land to loyal Norman lords ensured that the new ruling class was dependent on the king for their wealth and power. William maintained the existing Anglo-Saxon legal system but introduced new laws and administrative practices that centralised power in the hands of the king and his officials.

Under the Anglo-Saxon system, earls were powerful regional lords who wielded significant authority in their respective territories. After the Conquest, William sought to diminish the power of earls by replacing them with a new group of Norman nobles who were more directly answerable to the king. Moreover, William divided their territories into smaller units called shires, which were governed by appointed officials known as sheriffs. These sheriffs, who were responsible for tax collection, law enforcement, and the administration of justice, reported directly to the king, thus limiting the influence of earls and further centralising power.

During his reign, William I spent considerable time outside England, particularly in Normandy, to maintain control over his continental territories. In his absence, he appointed regents to govern England on his behalf. Regents, who were usually close relatives or trusted advisors, held significant authority and were responsible for overseeing the administration, maintaining order, and ensuring the king's interests were protected. One notable regent during William's reign was his half-brother, Odo of Bayeux, who served as both the Bishop of Bayeux and the Earl of Kent. Odo played a crucial role in maintaining stability in England, particularly during the years of rebellion and unrest following the Conquest. However, his ambitions eventually led to his fall from grace, as he was arrested and imprisoned by William in 1082 for plotting against the king.

The Norman Conquest led to significant changes in the government of England under William. The centralisation of power, the limited use of earls, and the role of regents were all key aspects of the new system of governance, which aimed to secure and maintain control over the newly conquered territory. These reforms laid the groundwork for the development of a more efficient and centralised government in England, which would continue to evolve in the centuries that followed.

Key Points:

- William introduced reforms to consolidate his power and control over the newly conquered territory.
- In contrast to the pre-Conquest decentralised Anglo-Saxon government, William established a more unified governance system with the monarchy at its core.
- By dispossessing Anglo-Saxon nobles and redistributing land to loyal Norman lords, he made the new ruling class dependent on the king.
- The king upheld the existing Anglo-Saxon legal system but implemented new laws and that further centralised power to himself and his officials.
- He diminished the power of the previously influential earls by replacing them with Norman nobles who were directly accountable to the king.

- William divided the earls' territories into smaller units called shires, each governed by appointed sheriffs responsible for tax collection, law enforcement, and justice administration.
- When abroad, William appointed regents to govern England in his stead; they held significant authority and were tasked with maintaining order and protecting the king's interests.
- One such regent was William's half-brother, Odo of Bayeux, who played a key role in stabilising England during years of rebellion, though he was later imprisoned for plotting against the king.
- The Norman Conquest brought about significant changes to England's governance, including centralisation of power, limited use of earls, and the use of regents.
- These reforms laid the foundation for a more efficient, centralised government in England, setting the stage for its further evolution in subsequent centuries.

Sheriffs and the Demesne

Before delving into the establishment and significance of the 'forest' in Norman England, we first need to understand the role of the sheriff during this era. The title "sheriff" comes from the Anglo-Saxon "shire-reeve", which literally means the guardian of the shire. During the late Anglo-Saxon period, the sheriff's responsibilities involved maintaining law and order, collecting taxes, and overseeing the local militia.

After the Norman Conquest in 1066, William retained the existing Anglo-Saxon administrative structure, including the office of sheriff. However, the role evolved significantly under Norman rule. Sheriffs were often appointed from the Norman aristocracy, often serving the dual role of local administrative authority and representative of the king. They were responsible for implementing royal directives, collecting royal revenues, supervising the legal system, and ensuring local security.

The demesne was a key feature of the Norman feudal system in England. It referred to the portion of land retained by a lord for his own use and support, rather than being given to tenants. The demesne could include farms, pastures, mills, woods and other resources. These lands were often worked by serfs or villeins, who owed their lord labour services in exchange for protection and the right to cultivate their own plots of land. The demesne system served as a fundamental mechanism for wealth extraction and control in the Norman feudal society. It enabled the Norman lords to generate income, maintain a workforce, and exert control over the rural population.

In the context of Norman England, the term 'forest' did not only refer to areas covered with trees and undergrowth. Instead, 'forest' denoted a legally defined area set aside for royal hunting. Forests were governed by a distinct set of laws, known as the Forest Law, which was separate from the common law of the land. These laws protected game animals and their habitats for the king's use.

The establishment of royal forests was one of the most controversial aspects of William's reign. These 'forests' often included villages and farmland, impacting local people's lives significantly. Many people were displaced from their lands without compensation. Hunting within these forests without royal permission was considered a serious offense, often leading to harsh punishments.

The 'forest' served multiple purposes for the Normans. Firstly, it asserted the King's dominance, as it was a clear reminder of his authority and power. Secondly, it contributed to the economy through fines imposed for forest law violations. Thirdly, it preserved the game for the leisure of the king and his court, reflecting the social elitism of the Norman aristocracy.

The office of sheriff, the demesne, and the 'forest' were key components of the administrative, economic, and social transformations that England underwent during the Anglo-Saxon and Norman period of 1060-1088. These elements highlight the consolidation of Norman power, the implementation of the feudal system, and the cultural changes introduced by the Norman conquerors.

Key Points:

- The title "sheriff" derives from the Anglo-Saxon term "shire-reeve", which signifies the guardian of the shire,
- Responsibilities included maintaining law and order, collecting taxes, and managing the local militia.
- Sheriffs under Norman rule were responsible for enforcing royal directives, collecting royal revenues, supervising the legal system, and ensuring local security.
- Demesne lands were often worked by serfs or villeins, who provided labour services to their lord in exchange for protection and cultivation rights.
- In Norman England, the term 'forest' was a legal designation for areas reserved for royal hunting.

- These areas were governed by special laws known as the Forest Law, which were separate from the common law of the land.
- Establishing royal forests was a contentious aspect of William's reign as these often included villages and farmland, displacing local people without compensation and imposing harsh punishments for hunting without royal permission.
- The 'forest' asserted the King's dominance, served as a source of income through fines for forest law violations, and preserved game for the king and his court, reflecting the social elitism of the Norman aristocracy.

The Domesday Survey

The Domesday Book is a critical primary source for understanding the societal and administrative structures of Norman England. Commissioned by William, this exhaustive survey was completed in 1086 and offers insight into the extensive systems of Norman government and finance.

In late 1085, King William I commissioned a detailed survey of England's wealth and resources. This came to be known as the Domesday Book. Its purpose was multifaceted; primarily, William needed an accurate record of the land's wealth to levy taxes effectively and also to understand who held what land, and how much it was worth. The Domesday Book was thus a tool to consolidate William's power and to maintain control over his new kingdom.

The Domesday Book is divided into two volumes: "Great Domesday" and "Little Domesday". Great Domesday covers most of England, excluding London, Durham, parts of the northwest, and most of East Anglia. Little Domesday provides a more detailed account of Essex, Norfolk, and Suffolk. The survey lists landowners, their holdings, and the resources tied to those holdings. It provides insights into the population, wealth, industry, and agriculture of Norman England.

The Domesday Book had significant implications for Norman governance. It provided a detailed record of land ownership, which was useful in settling disputes and enforcing feudal obligations. With this information, the King could assert authority over his vassals more effectively. Additionally, the Domesday Book served as a benchmark for the King's legal and financial control over the country. It provided comprehensive data that underpinned the fiscal, judicial, and military systems of Norman governance.

The Domesday Book was crucial to the financial administration of Norman England. It provided a definitive record of taxable wealth and resources. Each entry included the value of the land, its assets, and the taxes owed. This allowed the King to levy taxes efficiently, contributing significantly to the royal treasury. Moreover, the Domesday Book's record of land and resource distribution helped the King control the English economy. Knowing the resources available in each area enabled the Normans to extract wealth strategically and maintain economic stability.

The Domesday Book was a critical instrument for Norman governance and finance. It offered a detailed record of land ownership and resources, allowing the Normans to exert control over England. The book served as a precedent for the government's collection of economic data, influencing practices of taxation and financial administration that are foundational to modern government systems. This survey of England was an extraordinary achievement for its time. It provides us today with an invaluable snapshot of Anglo-Saxon and Norman England between 1060 and 1088, acting as a cornerstone of English administrative history.

Key Points:

- The Domesday Book is a crucial primary source for understanding Norman England's societal and administrative structures.
- It was completed in 1086.
- The survey was done to record England's wealth and land distribution.
- This enabled efficient tax collection, consolidated William's power, and maintained control over his kingdom.
- The Domesday Book is divided into "Great Domesday" and "Little Domesday", the former covering most of England, while the latter provides a detailed account of Essex, Norfolk, and Suffolk.
- The information contained in the Domesday Book includes listings of landowners, their holdings, and associated resources.
- The detailed record of land ownership in the Domesday Book was significant for Norman governance as it helped in dispute resolution, enforcing feudal obligations, and asserting the King's authority.

- It provided a definitive record of taxable wealth and resources, which facilitated efficient tax collection and economic control.

3.3 – The Norman Aristocracy

Culture and Language

When William, the Duke of Normandy, ascended the English throne after the Battle of Hastings in 1066, he brought with him a Norman aristocracy that transformed the cultural and linguistic landscape of England. This group, originating from northern France, introduced new traditions, customs, art, and architecture. Crucially, they brought a dramatic shift in language, moving from the Old English spoken by the Anglo-Saxons to the Old Norman dialect of French.

Norman culture was characterised by a distinct blend of Viking and French influences, given their roots as Norsemen who had settled in the region of Normandy in the 10th century. Their customs were considerably refined compared to the Anglo-Saxons', with a heavy emphasis on feudal principles, chivalry, courtly manners, and art. The Feudal System, already established in Normandy, was introduced to England. It characterised the relationship between the King, his vassals (nobles), and their sub-vassals, ensuring loyalty through a series of mutual obligations and protection. Norman knights were expected to abide by the code of chivalry, which highlighted virtues such as bravery, courtesy, honour, and gallantry towards women. This chivalric code influenced the conduct at the royal court, where etiquette and manners were highly valued.

The Normans introduced the Romanesque architectural style, most notably visible in cathedrals, castles, and abbeys. The Tower of London and Durham Cathedral are classic examples. They also brought with them a rich tapestry tradition, of which the Bayeux Tapestry, depicting the events leading up to the Norman conquest of England, is a renowned artifact.

The Normans spoke Old Norman, a Romance language derived from Latin, significantly different from the Germanic Old English of the Anglo-Saxons. As the Normans took control of the English elite, their language began to permeate English society. The Norman Conquest marked a transition from Old English to Middle English. Old Norman heavily influenced the English vocabulary, especially terms related to law, government, arts, and high culture. For example, words like "court," "justice," "art," and "army" have Norman roots.

The elite, composed of the monarchy, nobility, and clergy, primarily used Anglo-Norman, a variant of Old Norman. This dialect was a mix of Old Norman and Old English elements, and it was used in English courts and official documents for several centuries, further blending the two languages. Although Old Norman became the language of the elite, Old English continued to be spoken by the general populace. Th s led to a society with a high degree of bilingualism, reflected in the linguistic development of English.

From 1060 to 1088 the Norman aristocracy significantly influenced English society, culture, and language. Their profound impact can still be seen today in the fabric of modern English language and the socio-political structures inherited from the feudal system.

Key Points:

- After the Battle of Hastings in 1066, William brought with him a Norman aristocracy that greatly transformed England's cultural and linguistic landscape.
- This aristocracy originated from northern France and introduced new traditions, customs, arts, and architectural styles.
- The Normans instigated a significant shift in language, transitioning from the Anglo-Saxons' Old English to the Old Norman dialect of French.
- Their customs were more refined than the Anglo-Saxons', emphasising feudal principles, chivalry, courtly manners, and arts.
- They introduced the Feudal System to England, a structure characterising the relationships among the King, his vassals

(nobles), and their sub-vassals, securing loyalty via mutual obligations and protection.

- Norman knights adhered to a chivalric code, embodying virtues such as bravery, courtesy, honour, and gallantry towards women, influencing the conduct at the royal court.
- Architecturally, the Normans brought the Romanesque style to England, evident in cathedrals, castles, and abbeys, such as the Tower of London and Durham Cathedral.
- The Norman Conquest marked the transition from Old English to Middle English, with Old Norman significantly influencing the English vocabulary, especially in law, government, arts, and high culture.
- While Old Norman became the language of the elite, Old English remained the language of the general populace, leading to a high degree of societal bilingualism.

Bishop Odo

Bishop Odo of Bayeux, also known as Odo de Conteville, was an important figure during the Norman Conquest and the subsequent rule of the Normans in England from 1060-1088. As the half-brother of William, Odo played a pivotal role in the events of this period.

Born around 1030, Odo was the son of Herleva of Falaise and her second husband, Herluin de Conteville. This made him the half-brother of William, who was Herleva's son from a previous relationship. Despite his lack of formal religious education, Odo was appointed Bishop of Bayeux in Normandy in 1049 when he was around 19 years old. This was an unusual move, likely motivated by William's desire to consolidate power within his family.

Odo played a key role in the Norman Conquest. He was instrumental in the preparation for the invasion, reportedly commissioning the construction of the "Mora", the ship that carried William to England in 1066. He is also depicted in the Bayeux Tapestry, a significant historical record of the era, rallying troops for the Battle of Hastings. Though not a fighting man due to his ecclesiastical status, Odo was present at the Battle of Hastings, offering spiritual and possibly strategic support. He is often credited with encouraging the feigned retreat tactic that led to the Normans' victory.

Following the successful conquest, Odo was granted substantial lands in England, making him one of the richest men in the country. He was appointed Earl of Kent in 1067 and served as William's deputy when the king was in Normandy. His rule, however, was characterised by harshness and greed, and he was accused of defrauding the crown and the church. This culminated in his imprisonment in 1082, supposedly for planning a military expedition to Italy.

Bishop Odo's significance in Anglo-Saxon and Norman England cannot be understated. His influence and actions in this period had profound effects on the politics, culture, and economy of England. As a close confidante of William, Odo was instrumental in consolidating

Norman power in England. His position as Earl of Kent gave him substantial authority, which he often used to suppress Anglo-Saxon uprisings.

Odo is widely believed to have commissioned the Bayeux Tapestry, an essential cultural artefact that provides a comprehensive visual account of the Norman Conquest. As a landlord, Odo also had a significant influence on the English economy. His management of his lands, although often heavy-handed, contributed to the establishment of the feudal system in England. Despite his secular activities, Odo's position as Bishop of Bayeux made him a crucial figure in the English Church. His appointment highlighted the changing power dynamics within the Church, with Normans replacing many Anglo-Saxon bishops.

Bishop Odo's career and activities significantly impacted Anglo-Saxon and Norman England, with effects felt both during his life and long after his death in 1097.

Key Point:

- Bishop Odo of Bayeux was a key figure during the Norman Conquest and the subsequent rule of the Normans in England from 1060-1088.
- He was the half-brother of William and played a crucial role in the events of this period.
- Odo played a pivotal role in the Norman Conquest, as he was responsible for the construction of the "Mora," the ship that transported William to England in 1066.
- Odo was given substantial lands in England, making him one of the country's wealthiest men.
- He was appointed Earl of Kent in 1067 and acted as William's deputy when the king was in Normandy.
- His rule was marked by harshness and greed, leading to accusations of defrauding the crown and the church.

- Odo was eventually imprisoned in 1082 for allegedly planning a military expedition to Italy.
- As a close confidante of William, he played a key role in consolidating Norman power in England, using his position as Earl of Kent to suppress Anglo-Saxon uprisings.

3.4 – The Norman Aristocracy

William and Robert

Known for successfully invading England and implementing Norman rule after his victory at the Battle of Hastings, William was a complex figure. A skilled warrior, a diligent ruler, yet also a stern and, at times, brutal monarch, William successfully established himself as the king of England following his conquest in 1066. Yet whilst William worked tirelessly to maintain his power over England he also experienced further challenges with his eldest son, Robert Curthose, who despite inheriting the Duchy of Normandy had a contentious relationship with his father.

William was a forceful and determined character, evident from his audacious invasion of England. His leadership skills, coupled with strategic acumen and a willingness to embrace new military technologies, helped him secure victory at Hastings. His traits were not only military; he also demonstrated effective administrative qualities, evident in his introduction of the Domesday Book and feudalism. However, William could be harsh and was often characterised by his ruthless suppression of opposition, evident in his response to various revolts, such as the Harrying of the North. Despite this ruthlessness, he also respected the religious institutions and worked to maintain peace with the Church throughout his reign.

William's relationship with his eldest son, Robert Curthose, was fraught with tension. William, apparently doubting Robert's abilities and temperament, initially did not designate him as his heir, causing friction between the two. In 1077, a family dispute escalated into open revolt. Robert, feeling insulted by his brothers and unsupported by his father, rallied a group of discontents and began a rebellion against William. This became known as Robert's Revolt and resulted in a three-year period of civil war in the Duchy of Normandy.

The revolt in Normandy from 1077 to 1080 was a significant conflict in William's later reign. Robert, having gained the support of several key nobles and King Philip I of France, waged war against his father. However, despite several battles, Robert failed to gain a decisive victory.

In 1080, the revolt effectively ended following the intervention of Queen Matilda, who brokered peace between father and son. Robert remained in control of Normandy but agreed to be William's vassal, effectively recognising William's superiority. This settlement remained in place until William's death in 1087.

The relationship between William I and Robert is a testament to the complex family dynamics and political tensions of the period. William, despite his strengths as a leader, faced significant challenges, not only from external threats but also from within his own family. Meanwhile, Robert's rebellion illuminates the power struggles inherent in the Norman succession and the volatile nature of feudal relationships.

Key Points:

- Despite his many accomplishments, William's rule was characterised by ruthlessness.
- Regardless of his harshness, William maintained a respectful relationship with religious institutions and endeavoured to keep peace with the Church during his reign.
- William's relationship with his eldest son, Robert Curthose, was filled with tension.
- William's initial reluctance to designate Robert as his heir fuelled friction between them.
- This tension escalated into open revolt in 1077 when Robert, feeling insulted and unsupported, rallied discontents and waged a rebellion against his father.
- The revolt in Normandy from 1077 to 1080, despite the support Robert received from key nobles and King Philip I of France, did not lead to a decisive victory for Robert.

- The revolt effectively ended in 1080 following Queen Matilda's intervention, which brokered peace between William and Robert.
- While Robert retained control of Normandy, he agreed to become William's vassal, recognising William's superiority.
- This settlement held until William's death in 1087.
- Robert's rebellion underscored the inherent power struggles in the Norman succession and highlighted the volatile nature of feudal relationships.

William's Death and the Disputed Succession

The succession to the throne following the death of William on September 9, 1087, was mired in controversy and conflict. William's eldest surviving son, Robert Curthose, should traditionally have inherited the English throne. However, William's preference for his second son, William Rufus, complicated matters. Before his death, William split his dominions, bequeathing Normandy to Robert and the English throne to William Rufus.

This divergence from the customary rules of succession, coupled with long-standing rivalries among his sons, sparked a power struggle that lasted for years. It is noteworthy to mention that William's youngest son, Henry, was bequeathed a large sum of money, but no lands. This would later set the stage for Henry's significant role in the affairs of England and Normandy.

William II, also known as William Rufus due to his ruddy complexion, was crowned King of England on September 26, 1087. Rufus's reign was plagued with challenges, notably from his elder brother Robert and their uncle Odo of Bayeux, the Bishop of Bayeux and Earl of Kent. Robert, feeling wronged by the distribution of their father's lands, was eager to claim England for himself. Odo, a powerful figure during William's reign, also sought to gain more power and influence. He was the main instigator of the Rebellion of the Earls in 1088, which was ostensibly launched in support of Robert's claim to the English throne.

William Rufus, however, proved to be a capable and ruthless leader. He quickly crushed the Rebellion of the Earls with the help of loyalists, which included Lanfranc, the Archbishop of Canterbury. His victory was decisive and significantly weakened the power of the rebellious earls, among them Odo of Bayeux, who was exiled back to Normandy. This victory solidified William Rufus's position as king, and he would continue to rule until his death in 1100.

The defeat of Robert Curthose was less straightforward. Robert and William were in a continuous state of conflict for much of their reigns, but Robert was never able to muster the resources or support needed to wrest England from his brother's control. While Robert did maintain his hold on Normandy, his power and influence were substantially diminished by his ongoing conflicts with William.

The period following William's death was characterised by internal strife and political manoeuvring, driven by disputes over the rightful succession and territorial disputes between William's sons. William Rufus's victory over his opponents not only consolidated his power in England but also shaped the course of English and Norman history for years to come.

Key Points:

- The succession to the throne following the death of William on September 9, 1087, was mired in controversy and conflict.
- William's eldest surviving son, Robert Curthose, should traditionally have inherited the English throne.
- However, William's preference for his second son, William Rufus, complicated matters.
- Before his death, William split his dominions, giving Normandy to Robert and the English throne to William Rufus.
- This divergence from the customary rules of succession, coupled with long-standing rivalries among his sons, sparked a power struggle that lasted for years.
- What followed was a disputed succession in which William and Robert went to war with one another.

Printed in Great Britain
by Amazon

26598230R00056